FOLLOW INSTRUCTIONS ON PAGE 85 TO VIEW PREPPERS VIDEOS!

SUMMARY

BOOK 4: USEFUL TOOLS IN EVERYDAY LIFE 46

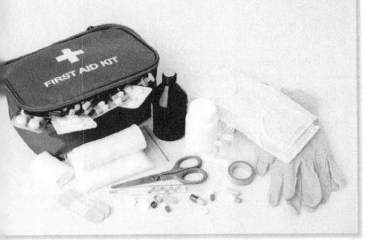

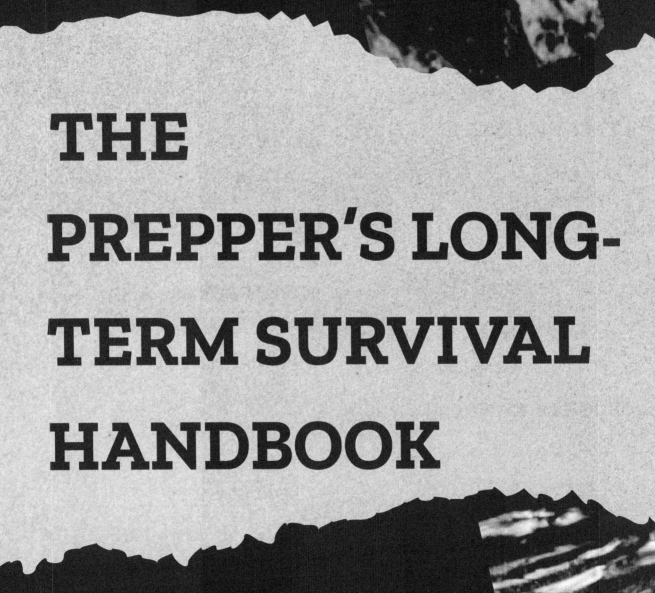

THE PREPPER'S LONG-TERM SURVIVAL HANDBOOK

Introduction

Who is the prepper? A prepper, according to the Cambridge Dictionary, is someone who believes that a way or disaster of some kind is going to happen soon. This person learns skills and collects equipment and food in order to help them prepare for this inevitable circumstance. A prepper is someone who knows that society and the world as we know it isn't going to last forever. We have seen the world around us break down time and time again. It's only logical that one would need to prepare for that moment where society will not be able to recover as it has done in the past.

Recent events have let us know exactly how unprepared we are. The rush to the store at the last second to gather all the supplies and food you might need because you don't know when the stores will be open again, if they ever do open again, is something you can avoid if you are prepared. This is more than just stockpiling on canned food and solar energy. This is more than basements filled with bottled water and fuel for generators. This is a lifestyle that could prepare you for the fallout that we all know is coming.

It seems like a waste of time at first. After all, you never really do know when disaster will hit. You may feel as though you can never really be prepared for something like that. Yet, we have seen time and time again how the unprepared suffer and the prepared are kept safe. It's the difference between running through a store on teh day it's going to close only to find all the shelves barren, or sitting comfortably at home knowing you have everything that you could possibly need for the foreseeable future.

Preparing yourself and your family for these emergencies can save both your and their lives. You need to learn how to survive when society crumbles. You need to be able to help yourself in times when there will be no help. This is what the prepper is. Someone who is capable of helping themselves and others in a time where no help is coming at all.

THE PREPPER'S LONG-TERM SURVIVAL HANDBOOK

 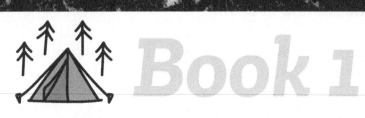 *Book 1*

Book 1:

Preparing Yourself and Your Family for SHTF

When disaster does hit, there is no way for us to know exactly how bad it is going to be. We can either be prepared for every possible outcome, or we can be left wondering what to do and how to survive.

We face many dangers on a daily basis, and the best thing to do is make sure both you and your family are prepared for when you eventually face something

that will change the way you live your life.

There are many ways you can prepare for disaster before it happens, and the steps you must take are simple but essential.

Step 1: Identify Risks in Your Area

Depending on the area you currently live in, you can be more or less at risk when disaster does strike. Your first step should be to identify the risks you face in your everyday life and in the area yo ulive. This includes your home, your work, and your neighborhood.

You might be at work when disaster does strike, so you need to assess the risk you'll be facing. If you work on a high floor of your building, you need to know all the exit points and how easy it will be to reach them. What hazards could you be facing? If the building isn't structurally sound, you might have to prepare a duck and cover maneuver if the roof caves in. All these things must be taken into account when you prepare. The same can be said for where you live. The same risks must be assessed and, if possible, avoided.

Another thing that needs to be taken into account is how far away your work is from your home. You need multiple planned routes for when disaster does strike so you can get to your home no matter what happens. Your routes home need to be planned around whatever disaster you might face, whether it be earthquakes, floods, or something man made.

Assessing the risks in your area comes next. Is your area prone to floods, or earthquakes, or is it hot and dry, which means there's more chance of a fire breaking out? Knowing these things will help you better prepare.

Step 2: Create a Plan and Practice It

Preparing yourself and your family for disaster involves creating a plan or strategy for when it does eventually happen. In this plan, everyone needs to be given a job or a set of steps to follow.

The most important steps will involve what to do and where to go when it happens.

Any good disaster plan involves taking immediate action after the fact and having a place for everyone to meet. You might be at work and your children might be at school when disaster strikes. The most important thing is making sure you all can get together if you are separated.

Your plan can involve meeting up inside your house, outside your house, or in another place entirely. This all depends on what disaster you are facing. It may be safer for your family to stay put until you can reach them, and it might be a better idea for them to leave their area and meet you somewhere safer.

All of this must be taken into account when planning for a disaster with your family. Once you've made a plan, you need to practice it. Treat it like a fire drill. Pick a day and a time to practice.

Everyone needs to memorize their steps and play it out as if it was an actual disaster. Only by practicing can you be sure that you and your family are prepared.

Step 3: Build a Disaster Kit

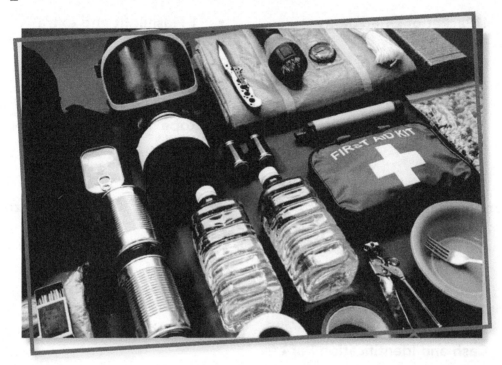

Building a disaster kit for your home and for your car will ensure that you will have everything you need on hand for any kind of disaster. Your disaster kit needs to be filled with essentials, stored in an easy to reach area, and light enough that even your children could carry it with ease.

It's hard to pack a disaster kit for any known disaster, but it's easy once you know the basic essentials that you'll need regardless of what happens.

It's important to have a disaster kit fully stocked and ready to be used. Having multiple disaster kits for different locations is also a good idea in case one location is blocked off. Everyone in your family should know the locations of the disaster kits and should be instructed to go for the safest one as soon as possible. As long as one of you gets a hold of one of these kits when disaster strikes, you'll be prepared for anything.

For your **Disaster Kit**, you'll need the next things:

- 1 Water Bottle for each person
- 2 Protein Bars for each person
- 1 Packet of Dried Jerky
- Pain Medication
- Bandages and Plasters
- Antiseptic
- 3 Day Supply of Nonperishable Food
- Can opener
- Matches in Waterproof Container
- Cash and Identification Papers
- Blankets

- Extra Clothing
- Whistle
- 1 Flashlight and extra Batteries
- A Radio
- Rope
- 1 Mask for each person
- A Pocket Knife or multi-tool
- A Roll of Duct Tape
- A Map of your area
- A Compass or GPS Device

Make sure there is room in your pack and in your plan to account for pets, toddlers or babies, and special needs persons. Not everyone will be able to prepare for disaster the same way, so make sure you accommodate those who need extra help.

Step 4: First Aid Training

You need to prepare for an event where help is not on the way. Your family members or yourself could be injured. You need first aid training in order to be able to help the injured or the trapped, because there will come a time when no one will come to help you.

First aid and CPR training is a must in these instances. You need to be able to react fast and know exactly what to do if you or someone else gets hurt.

STRATEGY AND PLANNING FOR PREPPERS

  **Book 2**

Book 2:

Strategy and Planning for Preppers

Planning and preparing yourself and your family for a disaster involves a lot more than just coming up with a plan and stockpiling for the day the shops close. You need a strategy, and you need to know everything that there is to know.

Knowledge and planning can mean the difference between life or death when it comes to any kind of disaster scenario.

Toughening Up

Any prepper will tell you that there are countless ways to prepare for a life-altering event. There are also some out there who will try to convince you that there is no way to prepare for something that might never happen. It's true that there is no way to know when something is going to happen, but that doesn't mean you can't be prepared for it. Recent events serve as proof that we need to be more prepared for when these events can and will happen.

Toughening up might seem like a broad subject, but it's a fairly simple concept. It is the act of preparing one's body and mind for the end of life as we know it. Stocking up on food and supplies, creating a strategy, and developing a plan for when 'stuff hits the fan' is not enough in the long run.

You may find yourself carrying a heavy bag through the woods, hiking to a safe destination, growing or sourcing your own food, or even just carrying large water bottles from your storage area to your living area. All these things require training. You can't just pack a bag filled with food and supplies and wait till the day that a disaster happens to bug out. Your body and mind won't survive the journey, no matter how prepared you might be.

Toughening up is a process that you need to go through in order to survive. There are several ways you can do this.

Daily Exercise

Strengthening your arms, legs, and core are essential to survival. Cardio, strength, and fitness training must be worked into your daily routine in order to maintain your physical health. If you consider yourself to be physically fit then maintenance is key. However, if you're not physically fit, it must be your number one priority to be so.

Simple exercises, such as jogging and jumping jacks, can add to your overall fitness and cardio, but strength training is the most important things you need to do. You don't need to become a bodybuilder or develop a six pack, but gaining a small amount of muscle tone can help you immensely.

BOOK 2

The exercises you should consider adding to your daily routine include:

- **Push-ups:** If you are unfamiliar with push-ups or have weak arms in general, then you should start slow with knee push-ups and work your way up.

- **Jogging:** Jogging gets your heart pumping and strengthens your lungs. Cardio is important because it tests your endurance.

- **Jumping jacks:** This gets the heart pumping and is a good alternative to jogging if you are unable to.

- **Sit-ups:** This can strengthen your core, which makes it easier to lift and carry heavy objects. If you're unable to do a full sit-up at first, you can start with crunches to strenghten the area first.

- **Mountain Climbers:** This is a full body workout that tests your strength as well as your endurance. Start out slow and build up in speed as you get stronger.

These are all simple exercises that you can do to strengthen your body, lungs, and heart. Endurance and strength can help you out there whether you choose

to bug out or bug in.

Before adding any of these exercises to your daily routine, be sure to discuss them with your doctor if you have any previous physical disabilities such as weak knees or elbows. Some exercises are unsafe and can end up weakening you instead. For instance, squats can end up damaging your knees if your upper body weight is too high and your leg muscles are too weak. If this is the case, your doctor can help you determine what exercises you can use to substitute.

Remember that survival is physically strenuous, and you can't make it if you aren't up to the challenge.

Gear Training

This is another way to prepare not just you, but also your gear for the disasters ahead. Most of us will buy survival supplies only to pack them away and wait till the moment we need them to use them for the first time. This is one of the worst mistakes you could make as a new prepper.

There's a lot that can go wrong when it comes to your gear. The first time you try

to set up a tent can be a trying task. Even if you follow the instructions, you can still mess up. Gear can malfunction, or you just might not understand how to properly use it. Training with your gear is the best way to make sure these mistakes never happen. There are three main reasons why you should train with your gear:

1. Learn to use your gear

In an event when bugging out is your only option, you don't want that to be your first time setting up your tent or using your camp stove. Take your gear for a test drive and get familiar with how it works.

2. It's physically strenuous

Your gear will be heavy, and you may find yourself walking or hiking for miles. Training with your gear gets your body used to carrying the weight of your supplies up hills, down long roads, and over challenging terrain.

3. To test out your gear

You may buy a piece of equipment that looks good, came highly recommended, or seemed suitable for your situation. However, when it comes down to it, that piece of equipment might not work well or might break down if under hard use. Training with your gear allows you to experience problems like your gear breaking down or not working the way you need it to before you actually need it to work. This gives you the opportunity to replace the gear with something more suitable ahead of time.

Survival Strategies

None of us truly know what surviving is until we're thrown into the thick of it and fighting for our lives. At any moment, the world that we know and the life we're used to living could be stopped in its tracks by a multitude of disasters and emergencies. Survival is about adjusting to any situation and living the best life that you can given your circumstances, but survival requires preparation and planning.

Survival strategies are things you can do now that will benefit you the day the

world as we know it comes crashing down around us.

Live Below Your Means

When disaster strikes, you won't have a choice but to change the way you live. You'll have to get used to eating less, keeping yourself entertained, and even living without hot or running water. These are luxuries that we cannot be certain will be available in a disaster scenario. That's why it's a good idea to try living without them now to prepare yourself for when you won't have a choice.

Living below your means now will prepare you for the days ahead when you'll be without simple luxuries or needs.

Off the Grid Living

Prepare yourself for living off the grid. This can be anything from learning to grow your own food to setting up a solar power grid for your home. Teach yourself how to forage for food in the wilderness. Don't expect to be the trapper and hunter you often see in the movies.

Wild game, whether it's small or large, is going to be hard to find if you end up in a situation where you run out of food. You can't expect to go hunting for deer or rabbits. Learn to live without that. By growing your own food, learning to forage for food, and even preparing yourself for snacking on insects can help you prepare for the world without canned and stored food.

Bugging Out or Bugging In

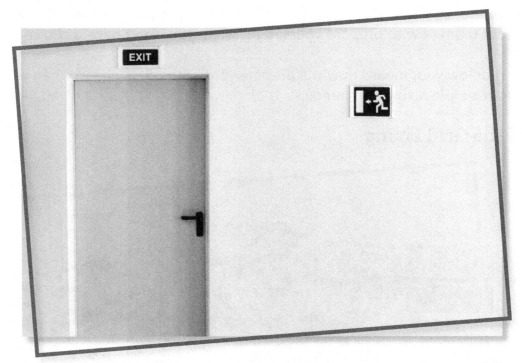

When it comes to the life of a prepper, you tend to prepare for two different situations; bugging out or bugging in. There has been an ongoing debate on which of the two is the best choice. Bugging in is a term used to describe a situation when disaster strikes and you choose to hole up inside your home and take shelter there. Bugging out is a term used to describe when you leave your home and either go to a secondary location or decide to camp out in the wilderness when disaster strikes. It's usually unclear which option is the best choice, but the most experienced prepper will prepare for both bugging out and bugging in.

A common mistake that new preppers make is focusing too much on bugging in or bugging out strategies instead of actually choosing which one they're going to do ahead of time. Bugging out and buggin in require specific situations, and there is no way to know what is going to happen.

You can't decide ahead of time, before a particular emergency happens, if you are going to be bugging out or bugging in. That kind of decision can only be made on the spot once you've received all the information you can get when disaster does strike.

Many new preppers tend to fantasize the idea of bugging out, and this is the main reason that they make the choice to do so. This is because when emergencies do happen, we have a primal urge to do something. It's not enough to just sit and wait. We have a need to survive, and often that need will tell us that we need to do something, even when doing nothing is the safest choice. This is why bugging out is the most made choice, even when it is the wrong choice.

This wouldn't be that bad a thing if it didn't stop people from preparing for both situations. Most people are so determined that when something happens they will bug out that they don't prepare their home for a situation where they have to stay in. They'll end up trapped in their homes with no food and no water.

The main question that is always raised in this situation is, "Do I bug out or do I bug in?" Unfortunately, there is no clear answer to that question. The best answer that any experienced prepper can give you is to prepare for both, but your home should be your default choice.

Bugging in will always be the safest option for many reasons:

1. **You know the area and the community.**

2. **You'll have more space to pack more supplies.**

3. **You usually have a right to defend yourself inside your own home, so you won't have to worry about using lethal force or weapons.**

4. **You know the escape routes and best defensive spots.**

5. **It's the best way to be found or contacted in emergency situations.**

6. **There are fewer unknown situations when surviving inside your home than surviving out in the wilderness.**

7. There could be factors making the outside more harmful or hazardous, such as sickness, gas, extreme weather conditions, toxins, ect.

There are still reasons to prepare for a **Bugging out** situation, such as:

1. The situation is unstable and unsafe due to fires, earthquakes, or floods causing damage to your home and the surrounding areas.

2. Civil unrest in or around your area causing a mob to form and begin looting and behaving violently.

3. The disaster happens while you're at work or away from your home and returning takes you over dangerous areas, or is unsafe in some way.

4. A known disaster is coming, such as a hurricane, and authorities have suggested that everyone in your area evacuate.

5. The supplies in your home are gone and there are none left in your immediate area.

Remember that when it comes to bugging out, that doesn't mean you have to be prepared to go live out in the woods or the mountains somewhere. A bug out location can be anything from a secondary home in the country, a friend or family's home out of the country, or even a bunker or trailer.

All of these make viable locations for bugging out. The main thing is that it is stocked with food, water, and supplies and that it is a safe area to escape to when your home is no longer safe.

As you can see, there are plenty of reasonable situations where you should either bug out or bug in. Both options are viable, which is why it is important to prepare for both. Stock up your home and prepare for the day you can't leave it. Find a predetermined destination and stock it up for the days where you simply can't stay at home.

THE PREPPER'S LONG-TERM SURVIVAL HANDBOOK

  # Book 3

Book 3:

Warming Up and Cooling Off

Exposure kills just as easily as a knife. When it comes to surviving in a disaster situation, knowing how to stay cool when it's too hot or warm up when it's freezing can save your life. In these technologically advanced days, we tend to rely on air conditioners and fans to keep cool and we cuddle up with our electric blankets and a mug of cocoa in order to keep warm. These are hardly going to be options during an emergency.

Learn to stay warm or keep cool when the elements are your worst enemy.

Warming Up

Freezing temperatures can lead to multiple effects on our bodies, the most extreme of which being frostbite, heart attacks, and hypothermia. Keeping warm can keep you alive and surviving. There are several ways you can easily heat up, or at least trick your body into heating up.

Focus Your Breathing

Something as simple as controlling your breathing can help you keep warm. Breathing in and out through your mouth can cool you down further. When you're feeling too cold, try breathing in and out through your nose. Breathe in and hold it for a few seconds, focusing on holding the warmth at the back of your throat. When you breathe out, do it in a slow and controlled way.

When we're cold, our first reaction is to breathe out air from our mouths onto our hands, but avoid this at all costs. This may warm up your hands, but it can cool down your lungs, and those are harder to keep warm than your hands are.

Dress Smart

Creating layers with your clothing can help trap heat and keep you warm. It's not just about creating layers, though; you have to wear the right clothing in the correct way.

You should have three layers for proper insulation. The first layer needs to be thin, thermal wear. Things like long johns or some kind of fast drying material. For the middle layer, you want thick material, like wool or fleece. Finally, for the outer layer, you want something that will protect you from rain, wind, and snow.

Make sure none of your clothes are too tight, because that can make you sweat, and sweating cools you down in the long run. When we sweat, we create moisture, and that moisture eventually cools down, creating a cold sweat. So, avoid wearing anything tight that can make you sweat and avoid any strenuous activity as well.

Lastly, cover every part of your body by wearing hats, gloves, and scarves.

Creating Friction and Huddling Up

You can target your pressure points, and by warming them up directly, you can affect your whole body's temperature. These pressure points are:

- **Wrists**

- **Temples**

- **Neck**

- **Ankles**

- **Elbow bends**

Targeting these points and creating friction can help warm you up immediately. Grab one of these pressure points and rub your fingers against it to create the friction.

Don't forget to huddle up! You can huddle up with yourself or with others. Our bodies give off heat, even in extreme cold. By huddling up by ourselves or with others, we can create a bubble of heat around our organs, preventing hypothermia and frostbite.

The bigger the mass is, the more heat it attracts. Tuck your arms underneath your shirt and pull your knees close to your chest. This should create a large enough mass that you generate more heat.

Eat Smart

You can eat and drink in a way that helps to warm you up as well. Most people make hot beverages such as tea, coffee, or cocoa in order to warm themselves up. We can assume that in most emergency situations, you won't be able to do this. However, you can boil water and slowly sip on a cup of it in order to mimic this act. Boiling the water also purifies it and makes it safe to drink.

You can also eat certain foods to warm you up. Ginger works as a stimulant. This means that it gets the blood pumping and circulating, which in turn raises your body's temperature. If you're able to stock up on ginger, you can nibble on a piece to warm yourself up.

Fatty foods can give you the same benefits. Fat is needed to insulate your body, and a low fat ratio in your body can lead to poor temperature regulation. Eating foods high in fat, like nuts, olive oil, and avocado can help you stay warm in colder weather.

Cooling Off

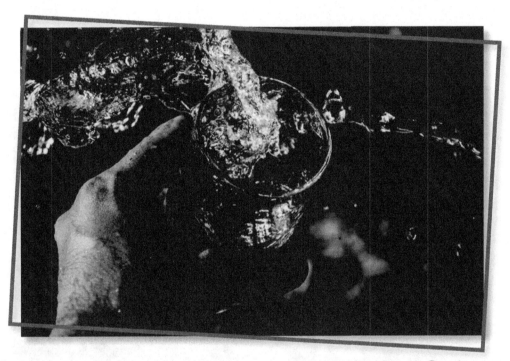

Cooling your body down is just as important as warming it up. Getting too hot can lead to extreme headaches and heat stroke. It's a lot harder to cool yourself down than it is to warm up, but there are a few tricks you can use.

Stay Hydrated

Drinking lots and lots of water is your best way to help your body maintain a decent temperature. Overheating can lead to dehydration, which can make it easier to get heat stroke.

Make sure to only drink liquid that hydrates you, so avoid drinks like coffee or anything salty. The drinks don't have to be cold either. Hot drinks can help you just as well as cold drinks.

Get Sweaty

Although sweating is an unappealing thing that our bodies do, it does have its purpose. Our bodies often sweat when we're hot or doing something strenuous. This is the body's way of cooling down. In other words, doing something strenuous can help your body sweat more, which cools you down faster.

Get Spicy

You might think that spicy food heats you up, but it tends to do the opposite. When you eat spicy food, you tend to sweat a lot. As mentioned before, this is your body's way of cooling you down. Eating something spicy is a safer way of cooling yourself off than just eating something that's hot.

THE PREPPER'S LONG-TERM SURVIVAL HANDBOOK

  *Book 4*

Book 4:

Useful Tools in Everyday Life

Buying the best and most expensive gear for your survival plan doesn't necessarily mean you're all set for when disaster strikes. Life is unpredictable, and so is any emergency. There are multiple things that can happen that will leave you trapped and unable to get to all that gear that you packed away for yourself.

An experienced prepper does not panic in this situation. Any prepper will know how to use any household items they have around them to get any job done. These are items that are common in any household, so you can be sure you'll have it on hand for when you'll need it.

Dental floss

Dental floss can be found in every household and is almost useful as rope. It's sturdy and easy to use. It might be a little more slippery than rope, but if you tie a knot with it, you can be sure it won't come undone. Dental floss can be use to rig snares, secure shelters, set up fishing lines, and to tie things down.

Chapstick

You might think that cosmetic items are the last thing you need to think about when in an emergency situation, but chapstick is one thing you're going to want to keep on you. It can be used for medical purposes such as placing it on cuts to stop the bleeding or bug bites to stop the itching. It can also be used to stop sunburn, and it's flammable enough to be used as a candle.

Empty chapstick containers can also be used as waterproof storage for small items like matches and pills.

Coffee filters

A coffee filter has many uses from hygienic to medicinal. It can be used as toilet paper in emergencies, a disposable bowl or plate, a bandage to stop bleeding, and it can even be used to filter debris from water sources. Make sure to boil any water afterwards because a coffee filter can remove harmful microorganisms.

Salt

This is the most important household item you can have in an emergency. Salt is a preservative, so you can rub it into food to make it last longer. Salt is also an antiseptic and can be placed on wounds to fight infection. Salt water can be gargled to help with sore throats, and salt can be placed on metallic surfaces to clean off rust before using them or create a non-stick cooking surface. It can also be used in the winter to melt away snow and add some traction to any slippery surfaces.

Paper clips

These office items are easy to twist and bend, but difficult to break. That means you can bend them to suit any purpose you need. They make excellent fishing hooks or needles. They can be used as lock picks and can even be linked together in order to create a makeshift chain.

Garbage bags

Garbage bags, especially heavy duty ones, can be very useful when it comes to waterproofing. They can be used for building an emergency lean-to or sealing shelters from wind and rain. They can be used as waterproof clothing by wearing it as a poncho or wrapping them around your shoes. They can also be used to collect and store water.

  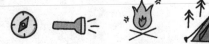

PREPPER'S
HOME DEFENSE

Introduction

If we're speaking statistically, this is the safest time in history to be alive. That doesn't mean that nothing bad is going to happen, and when it does, you need to protect not only yourself, but also your home.

A prepper's number one priority is home defense, but for new preppers it is an often overlooked step. Your home is where all your survival supplies are being stored. Your home is where you and your family will take shelter during an emergency or life-altering event. Your home is your most important asset on your prepping journey.

When something happens, and you've chosen the path of a prepper because you do believe that something can/will happen, your home is going to be your first line of defense. Your home is also going to be the biggest target. Emergenccies and life-altering events bring with them looters, thieves, and people desperate to survive. This is why it is important to know how to defend your home and property from anyone and everyone out there.

  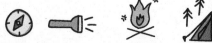

PREPPER'S HOME DEFENSE

  *Book 5*

Book 5:

Home Defense Perimeter

If someone wants to get into your home badly enough, you can bet that they will find a way. Setting up a defense perimeter is your best chance at defensing your home from those wanting to get inside.

Preppers know that survival means expecting the worst of every situation and preparing for it. The worst situation here being that someone has spotted your home and is looking to break into it. You can't know when it's going to happen or where they're going to come from. This is where a defense perimeter comes in handy.

Defensive Deterrents

When it comes to defensing your home, the first place to start is with deterrents. Deterrents go side by side with home defense. A deterrent is a great way of fixing the problem before it has a chance to become one. Ideally, you want to deter someone from even trying to break your perimeter.

If anyone is trying to break into your home, you want to make it more of a challenge. The more challenging your home looks, the more likely anyone wanting to break into it will change their mind and move on.

Signs

It's likely that anyone thinking about breaking and enetering is going to be casing your home first. They'll be looking for anything that can tell them how easy of a target you are. You want the first thing they see to be one or a few signs. These signs should warn them off of their plans to break into your home.

Signs like "smile, you're on camera," "beware of dog," "house protected by alarm," or "gun owner inside" will make the world of a difference when someone is casing your home.

It doesn't matter if the signs are true. You can hang a sign warning passersby of dogs without actually owning any dogs. The point is to make anyone who is looking think that there is a big, dangerous dog waiting to defend your home. It's unlikely that anyone reading the sign is going to wonder if it's true or not.

Hang these signs up at the front of your property so they are the first things that anyone sees.

Dogs

As mentioned above, you can have a sign warning passersby of dogs, or you can actually have a dog sitting right in front of your home. Dogs are like cheap security guards. All you have to do is feed it, keep it healthy, keep it happy, and make sure it's trained to protect you and your home.

BOOK 5

Dogs are great deterrents and alarms. The bigger your dog is, the bigger the deterrent it creates, but small dogs can still be useful and effective. Even if you can't own a dog, you can make it look like you do. Put a dog house in your yard and make sure it's visible. You can scatter dog toys around your yard, and a sign warning of a dog on the premises can be enough to fool anyone. Keep in mind that if you don't own a dog then all of this is simply a bluff and won't help if someone decides to try their luck.

Fencing and Gates

Building a fence around your perimeter is a great way to block off your property from the world. Fencing creates a physical barrier around your property and lets people know that if they cross that line, they are officially trespassing.

However, if someone wants to get onto your property, a fence or wall isn't going to stop them. A simple fence creates a physical barrier and acts like a deterrent. It isn't going to stop someone who is willing to climb over it. There are options, such as electric fencing, spikes, and barbed wire, that can create even more of a deterrent.

Driveways or paths through your front yard leading straight to a main road and connecting with a street can be a huge security problem. There's nothing stopping someone who's just walking down the street from wandering onto your property. Unless you have a gate. Gates go hand in hand with fences to protect your property and create a physical barrier.

Lights, Cameras, and Motion Sensors

Motion sensors and motion activated lights can be an effective deterrent. Most people wanting to break into your home are going to love the cover of dark. While having a light constantly shining on the outside of your property will take away their cover, a motion activated light will be far better.

These motion activated lights will lure any lurkers into a false sense of security. Once the light is activated, they'll be like a deer caught in headlights, and you'll receive a warning that someone has breached your perimeter. The lights should be blinding and pointed in a way where it will shine directly in the face of any intruders.

Motion sensors can be set up to warn you or set off a loud alarm to scare off any intruders. Any motion sensors should be placed as close to the entrances of your perimeter as possible. You don't want an intruder to get too close to your house before you receive a warning that they're there.

Security camera offer multiple benefits as a home defense tactic. They create a deterrent if they're placed in a visible area, they act as an early warning system for you, and they can be used to record any evidence if you ever get the chance to bring up an incident with law enforcement.

There are several options when it comes to security cameras. A full home security system is extremely expensive these days. These dummy cameras are a cheap option. They act as a visible deterrent. If an intruder believes they're being recorded or watched, they'll be less likely to continue with their plans. This ring doorbell camera is inexpensive and a light deterrent, but you can't expect that an intruder is going to be coming to the front door.

There are multiple options when it comes to cameras, and it's just about making the right choice for you and your home.

Defensive Landscaping

The landscaping in your yard, if done correctly, can act as your first line of defense against intruders. Along with your existing fence and gates, adding bushes, shrubs, hedges, and other plants to your can strengthen your defense. These act as extra obstacles and make your home even more of a challenge.

Although not always pleasing to the eye, there are many plants that grow thorns and spikes that will create a great deterrent to intruders. If an intruder managed to climb over your wall and landed in a bush full of thorns or spikes, they would begin rethinking all their life choices.

Keep any pets and children in mind if you decide to use this strategy. You wouldn't want your defense perimeter to become a hazard to your family.

PREPPER'S HOME DEFENSE

  *Book 6*

Book 6:

Window and Door Security

When it comes to keeping your home safe from intruders, your first concern should be the main points of entry. In other words, your windows and doors should be secure. The average home will contain up to 3 doors. A front door, back door, and side or sliding glass door. The average home also contains around 10 windows and a garage door. These are all your points of entry that you need to be concerned about.

Most intruders get into your house either through the doors, windows, or garage door, so these should be your priority when it comes to securing your house.

Door Security

You'll most likely have between 3 and 4 doors to consider when it comes to door security. Your front door is the main point of entry, so you might want to make it your first priority. However, most intruders tend to use the back door as an entry point because it is out of the way and less likely to be secure. Both the back and front door should receive the same amount of attention when you're setting up your home security.

Side doors and glass sliding doors are the most vulnerable points of entry. Most intruders prefer to enter a home quietly, but if given no other choice, they can easily break a glass sliding door and gain entry that way. Side doors also tend to be weaker and easy to break. These are huge concerns when it comes to your home's security.

A garage door often goes overlooked, but an intruder won't pass it up as an option to enter your home. Garage doors rarely have locks, and if they do, the locks are easy to bypass. Door security is a top priority in your home defense strategy.

Front and Back Doors

There are multiple steps you can take to secure your front and back doors, which act as main entry points for intruders.

1. Solid wood or metal doors

Exterior doors, such as your front and back door, should be made out of solid wood or metal. Most exterior doors in modern homes are made like this, but you'll find more often than not that your front or back wooden door is hollow. Replacing your front and back doors to solid wood or metal can be a first step in securing your home.

2. 3.5" screws

The front and back doors in average homes are usually held in place with short screws. These are fragile and easy to break, which means a desperate intruder won't find it difficult to rip your door off its hinges. Replacing the screws on the hinges and the strike plate to 3.5" screws will strengthen them and prevent this from happening.

3. Install deadbolts

Alongside your door's actual lock, you can install quality deadbolts to strengthen its security.

4. Form locking habits

We tend to make sure our doors are firmly locked and secured each night before we go to sleep. However, we can always expect that an intruder can strike at any time, not just when we're asleep in bed. Forming good locking habits can prevent an intrusion at all times.

Make sure to close and lock your doors whenever you leave the house or if you are inside. Even if you're only leaving the house for a moment to get the mail, or if you're at home in the middle of the day, always make sure all your doors are locked and secured.

Glass Sliding Doors

If you have a glass sliding door in your home, you may find it difficult to secure. It's basically a big window, which makes it tricky to turn into a secure area. However, there are multiple options when it comes to securing your glass sliding door against intruders.

1. Security locks

Most sliding doors come with only a simple latch to keep it locked and secured. By installing one of these security locks on your glass door, you can further deter any intruders and strengthen security.

2. Door jammer

A door jammer can add extra security to your sliding door and make sure intruders have a hard time breaking through.

3. Glass vibration and break detector

Installing this glass vibration and break detector to your glass sliding door is not a prevention measure, but it can serve as an early warning system. If an intruder does try to break through your glass sliding door by smashing the glass, this will alert you with an alarm.

4. Curtains and blinds

You can further discourage intrusion through a glass sliding door by hanging curtains and blinds and keeping them closed when you're not around. This will prevent anyone from being able to see inside your home. Most intruders won't even think about breaking into a home unless they can clearly see what's inside. The curtains or blinds create a mystery that can put off intruders.

5. Security film

Security won't stop an intruder from entering through your glass sliding door, but it can make it harder for them to enter by breaking it. Once you install security film on your glass sliding door, the glass won't shatter or break easily.

Window Security

The biggest challenge when it comes to home defense are windows. All of the windows in your house are the most vulnerable points of entry for any intruder. They're easily breakable, provide entry into nearly every room in the house, and usually have weak locks. That being said, there are plenty of ways you can secure your windows and strengthen them against intrusion.

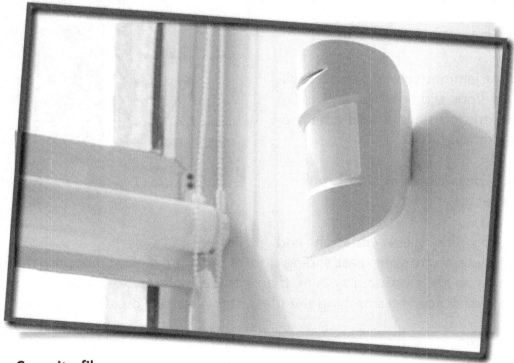

1. Security film

As mentioned above, as with glass sliding doors, security film can make it difficult for an intruder to break through glass. It stops it from shattering and can be applied to all your windows.

2. Metal screens

Most windows will have a nylon screen over it. Nylon screens are flimsy and easily torn. You can replace the nylon screens on your windows with stronger metal screens in order to improve their security.

3. Better locks

Most intruders will attempt to enter your home silently first before smashing through a window. Modern homes tend to have weak locks or latches on their windows, and these aren't going to stop any intruder with enough determination. Replace the locks on all your windows with strong quality locks.

4. Motion sensors and alarms

These motion sensors and window alarms can be a great early warning system. If any intruder attempts to break in through a window, it would set off a loud alarm, alerting you and making the intruder run for the hills.

5. Curtains and blinds

As mentioned above, in the glass sliding door section, intruders are more likely to break into your home if they can see what's inside it. Making sure your windows have blinds or curtains and that they are in use is a surefire way to warn away any intruders from looking into your home and seeing something they like.

PREPPER'S HOME DEFENSE

  **Book 7**

Book 7:

Bedroom and Night Security

Everything you've done up to this point has been to protect your house and everything inside of it. Your property is important to you, which is why you would go to such lengths to protect it. However, it's just as important to protect yourself and your family.

Alarms and cameras can warn you when someone has entered your home or is trying to. What is there to protect you in the night when an alarm doesn't sound? If you go to bed for the night, are you going to lie awake, wondering if an intruder is planning to sneak into your bedroom, or are you going to sleep soundly knowing that you are protected and prepared?

Night security and bedroom safety involves making sure your bedroom and those of your family are secured. Protecting your property and everything you own is important, but nothing is more important than our family.

Escape Plan, Safe Room, and Other Tips

If someone has breached your home in the night when you are sleeping or in your bedroom then your tactics need to change. At that point, it becomes more about survival. That means you don't have to be ready to confront the intruder or do something about it. Hiding or escaping your home in order to find help can be your only options, and there is no shame in this. Defending your home is important, but protecting your family should come first.

Escape Plan

An escape plan should be set up the moment you have your home defense system put in place. Escape plans are usually used as a last resort. If you need to use an escape plan, that means that an intruder has breached your home and you have no other option.

A successful escape plan needs only two things:

1. **An escape route**

2. **A destination**

If you have these two things, then all you have to do is design your plan and make sure everyone in your family knows it.

It's a good idea to have multiple escape routes selected. These should be near or in your bedroom and should be hidden to anyone but you. Having more than one escape route helps if, say, one of them is blocked to you by your intruder. Let's say your escape route is your bedroom window. If your intruder has an accomplice waiting at your bedroom window then you can no longer use it to escape. This is where having a second or even third option comes in handy.

An escape route must lead you out of your home in a safe and inconspicuous manner. An intruder should not be able to detect that you are aware of their presence in your home and making a move. Escape routes should lead to an area where you have easy access to a main road or a neighbor's property.

This brings us to the destination part of your escape plan. When you escape from your home, you need somewhere to go. If you're escaping your home due to an intruder, then you need to find help from someone else. A destination needs to include a place that you trust and a person who can help you.

A trusted neighbor's house is usually everyone's first choice for a destination. This or a nearby police station. You can even make your destination your car so you can speed away before your intruders know what is happening. From your destination, you can make your next move, which is to get help.

BOOK 7

Once you've designed an escape plan and set up your escape routes, you need to discuss it and practice it with your family. Everyone should have their own escape routes and know where to meet up. Practice makes perfect, so practice, practice, practice.

Safe Rooms and Hiding Places

Sometimes escaping your house during a home invasion might not be an option. This can be for many reasons, the main of which being that your escape route or your destination is unavailable. In this instance, it is best to avoid confronting the intruder and find a place where you'll be safe.

Safe rooms or hiding places can be anywhere in your house. A safe room is usually installed inside your bedroom. This makes it easy to access and a safe place to escape to without alerting the intruder. However, safe rooms are expensive to purchase and difficult to install.

Hiding places are a great alternative for anyone who is unable to afford or install a safe room. You can make a hiding place out of anything. A simple cupboard that is made out of solid wood or metal and can be locked from the inside can make a perfect hiding place from an intruder.

All hiding places need to be made of strong and hard material with high quality locks on the inside. This will stop an intruder from attempting to get inside your hiding place. Hiding places should be placed close to you and preferably inside your bedroom. They should also be as unnoticeable and inconspicuous as possible. As mentioned above, a cupboard makes for a perfect hiding place as it can be placed in a corner and might not draw an intruder's eye.

Each member of your family should have their own hiding place to escape to if your escape plan isn't an option.

Tips and Tricks

- There are many ways to protect yourself from any intruders entering your home in the dead of night. Forming good habits and practicing good security on a daily basis can help protect you and your family if you find yourself in the middle of an unfortunate situation.
on a daily basis can help protect you and your family if you find yourself in the

- Close and lock bedroom doors each night when you go to bed.

- Always close and lock windows while sleeping.

- Make sure curtains are drawn during the night.

- Leave at least one light on inside the house to give the impression that someone is still awake.

- Try leaving a television on and set to a low volume.

- Don't fall into a routine that is easily noticeable (i.e. always turning off all the lights and going to bed at the same time each night).

- If you're going out for the night, make sure you let a trusted neighbor know your house will be empty and make sure to leave a few lights on so it does not appear empty.

These small tips and tricks can help you prevent an intrusion so you never have to live through one, but never get complacent. An intruder can enter your home at any time of the day and at any day of the week. Preparation is your only defense.

PREPPER'S HOME DEFENSE

  *Book 8*

Book 8:

Weapons and Traps

When someone believes that their livelihood is under attack, their first instinct is to defend it. When someone breaks into your home and threatens to take away everything you've worked for, you want to be able to fight back and protect your property.

Escape routes, safe rooms, and defensive tactics work for some, but for others, the only option is to attack.

There are two different offensive tactics that you can use; direct attacks with weapons, and indirect attacks with traps. Each tactic has its advantages and disadvantages, and each tactic is a surefire way to defend your property and make

your intruder regret every decision they have ever made.

We're usually encouraged not to take the law into our own hands and to trust the protection of our lives and our property to the professionals. However, in a situation when no help is coming and you're on your own, which is what happens in most emergencies, you have to know how to take care of business yourself.

Traps

A trap is a device that is meant to detect an intruder, scare, and injure them. Traps can be made to fatally wound an intruder, but since self defense laws can be confusing, it's best to make all your traps to only scare or injure an intruder and not kill.

On your property, you can place alert-based traps and traps to incapacitate anyone wanting to invade your privacy. It's essential to keep all your traps to the non-threatening and non-lethal type during normal times. However, during situations where it is your life or theirs, then all bets are off.

Alert-Based Traps

Your priority should be traps that alert you to the intruders entering your premises. These traps should be loud and noticeable from anywhere on your property. They are meant to either scare off your intruder or warn you in time to prepare for their arrival.

Alert-based traps to be placed as close to the edge of your perimeter as possible. They need to be the first thing an intruder will pass when entering your property. They should be well hidden and placed at every possible entrance.

1. **Sound grenade trap**

This trap is simple to set up. First you'll need:

- **Sound grenades**

- **Thin tripwire**

THIN TRIPWIRE   **SOUND GRENADES**

When you have these things, all you need to do is measure the length of the entrance where you want to set up the trap. Cut a length of tripwire that is slightly longer than the area. Tie one end of the tripwire around the pin of the sound grenade and the other end to an anchored object, like a tree stump or rock. Tie some more tripwire around the other end of the sound grenade and then anchor that to a solid object on the opposite end of the entrance.

The tripwire should be pulled tight and at ankle or shin height. You don't want it to be easily noticeable, but if you put it too low, an intruder might be able to walk over it. Tripwire that is naturally colored can help camouflage it more.

Once an intruder walks through the trapped area, the pin will be pulled and the sound grenade will emit a 130 dB siren. This is loud enough to alert you to the intruder and even confuse them for a moment.

2. Air horn trap

This trap is a little more complicated, but it is cheap and quick to set up. First you'll need:

- **An air horn**

- **Thin tripwire**

- **A short, thick stick**

- **A heavy rock**

Once you have all these items, measure out the area where you want to set up your trap and cut a length of the tripwire that is slightly longer. Tie the one end of the tripwire around an anchored object, like a tree or a rock, and tie the other end around your stick. Once again, make sure the tripwire is set at ankle or shin height, pulled tight, and is naturally colored to hide it.

Dig a slight hole in the ground on the end of your entrance that is opposite the end where you have anchored your tripwire. Place the air horn in the hole with the trigger facing up towards the sky. Place your rock over the air horn and prop it up with your stick. Make sure the side of the rock over the air horn is flat. Now, when the trap is set off by an intruder walking through the tripwire, the stick will be pulled from its place, dropping the rock. The rock will push down the trigger on the air horn, setting off an alarm loud enough to scare your intruder and alert you.

3. **Door stop trap**

This trap is extremely simple and requires only one thing:

4. **A door stop alarm**

This item can be placed by any door to your property. A door stop alarm is a good alternative for anyone who can't afford a good alarm system.

When placed at a door and turned on, a door stop alarm will emit an ear-piercing alarm when a door is opened and pressed over it. There are different intensity settings for the alarm, the highest being loud enough to cause a sharp pain in an intruder's ear canal.

This is a great and simple way to momentarily incapacitate an intruder at your door and warn you of their presence.

BOOK 8

Outdoor Booby Traps

Aside from alerting you to the presence of an intruder on your property, traps can be used to literally trap someone. Incapacitating an intruder can be simple, safe, and effective in defending your property and protecting yourself. This is your best option in using traps to defend your property since most laws make it illegal to wound or kill anyone on your property with traps.

1. The Classic Pit Trap

This trap is simple and only requires some physical labor to set up. It's best used on large property with foliage so it can blend in.

You'll need a shovel so you can dig a hole in the ground that is at least six feet deep. This is deep enough to trap an intruder but not deep enough to cause any serious injury to the person that falls inside. You want the hole to be wide to avoid someone pushing up against the walls to climb out. Make sure the walls are smooth and flat, and that there is nothing to grab onto.

Once you have your pit ready, you can cover it with some foliage. Make sure you mark the area so you or your family members don't accidentally fall into the hole.

2. Spike Board Trap

A trap such as this one is easy to set up and is an excellent discouragement both physically and visually. For this trap, simply hammer some long or short nails into a wooden board. Lay the board flat in front of any entrances to your property, even on windowsills or in front of doors.

An intruder might not see this trap and wind up stepping on it. If they do that, they'll get a large nail stabbing them in the foot and they're likely to think twice about continuing onto your property and risking further injury. If an intruder spots your trap, it could have the same effect. They might wonder what lengths a homeowner who places spike boards around their property would go to in order to defend their home and leave before risking what else you have in store for them.

As with most traps, it's best to warn your family members about the locations of

these so you don't have any unintentional injuries.

Weapons

All your defenses have failed and an intruder has entered your house. You can't get out and you can't hide. The only thing left to do now is defend yourself and protect your home. However, that doesn't necessarily mean you have to grab your gun and start shooting.

There are nearly 5000 home burglaries per a day in America, and many of these occur while the homeowners are actually home. This is frightening, and this statistic has many homeowners rushing out to purchase themselves a firearm. This is all well good and well in theory, but many who purchase a firearm never consider the fact that if they use it, they actually might end up killing someone.This may be an effective way to defend your home from intruders, but not everyone is capable of that and might freeze on the spot. This can be more dangerous than not having a weapon at all.

Non-lethal self-defense weapons are easy to get a hold of and a far better choice for anyone who isn't quite ready to carry the death of someone else on their conscience. When bringing up the subject of a weapon for self-defense there are several points you need to consider:

- **Distance**

- **Damage**

- **Intimidation**

- **Convenience**

You should assume that an intruder is prepared to defend themselves as well. This is where the distance comes in. You want a weapon that doesn't require you to get too close to your intruder. Putting yourself at risk by getting too close should be avoided at all costs.

The damage comes in when you consider how useful your weapon is in combat.

You might not want to risk killing an intruder, but that doesn't mean you shouldn't try to harm them. Picking a weapon that is all bark and no bite won't do you any good. Humans instinctively avoid anything that can cause them pain. Psychologically speaking, humans avoid pain because we all have a natural instinct to live. This means that we tend to avoid any dangerous situations. Basically, just being intimidating enough can distract or dissuade your intruder. The suggestion of physical pain could be enough to frighten them away.

Convenience is considered when you think about how easy it is to keep your self-defense weapon near or on you. The best weapon is one that you have on you. That way, if an intruder enters your house in the dead of night and you're barely awake, you want your weapon to be within your reach before you even get out of bed. With those points in mind, here are a few non-lethal self-defense weapons to think about.

Pepper Spray

Pepper spray is simple but extremely effective. It can be used at a distance, can temporarily blind your intruder, and it stings enough to make them reconsider their plans. It's one of the most trusted non-lethal forms of self-defense. It's been used for years, and even the military and law enforcement have it as part of their arsenal.

This pepper spray is the favorite choice of the US Marshals, Chicago PD, and the NYPD.

Baton

A baton is another favorite choice of law enforcement and military forces. When fully extended, most batons can reach up to 21", helping you keep a safe distance from your intruder. Batons are also made of lightweight steel, meaning it doesn't require a lot of strength to swing it and still hits with devastating force. Batons are also convenient because, when collapsed, they can fit in a nightstand or kitchen drawer.

Baseball Bat

Most baseball bats work great as a self-defense weapon. They've even become a well known trope in Hollywood movies. Everyone always grabs a bat from underneath their bed and prepares to defend their home. This isn't just movie material. Baseball bats make excellent choices for self-defense weapons. They put a lot of distance between you and your intruder, they hit hard, and they're easy to get a hold of.

Stun Baton

If you've ever been electrocuted, or have seen videos of others receiving a little shock, then you know just how effective it can be. This stun baton can effectively drop a large, healthy man to the floor. It will help keep some distance between you and your intruder while delivering a disabling shock to them.

Keep in mind that repeatedly striking your intruder with this weapon could damage it, and the shock alone should be used as a warning.

OFF-GRID LIVING

Introduction

With the world's carbon footprint constantly rising, many have taken it upon themselves to change the way that humans live on this earth. Off-grid living is a side effect of this new movement, but preppers have been doing it for a lot longer.

Off-grid living is leaving the modern world behind, along with all of its conveniences and comforts, and learning to survive on your own. After all, experienced preppers understand that all of these modern conveniences and comforts are always going to be available to us. It's best to learn how to live without them now, before you have no choice.

With off-grid living, understanding all the things you need to survive is the key. You may think that you need electricity to survive. While it does make life easier, it's not really considered a necessity.

The three basic requirements that every human needs to survive are:

- **Shelter**

- **Food**

- **Water**

If you have these, then you can survive. However, we don't just want to survive. We want to live. Off-grid living is far more difficult and requires a lot more work, but it's not impossible to do.

  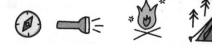

OFF-GRID LIVING

  *Book 9*

Book 9:

Constructing Your Shelter

Food and water are seen as essentials when it comes to survival, but the elements can be just as deadly as hunger and thirst. Having something to eat and some water to drink is good, but it means nothing if you don't have shelter. A shelter is more important than anything, and knowing how to construct on or find one when you're trying to survive can be the difference between life and death.

There are many types of shelters, whether they be permanent or temporary. Each shelter comes with its own benefits and its own hardships. Creating a shelter is a hugetask , but there are many ways you can go about it.

Underground Shelter

When it comes to underground survival, we mostly reference underground bunkers that were used during air raids in the war. Some old houses come with these already constructed, or you'd expect to pay a pretty penny to have one built for you. This isn't necessarily true. There are plenty of ways to get yourself an underground shelter to survive off-grid.

Build a Bunker

Building a bunker is no easy task, but if you know what you're doing, it can be done in 9 simple steps.

Step 1: Get permits

Building a bunker requires permission for several things, and this is the most important part. You need permits in order to build your bunker and in order to make it liveable. In order to get these permits, you will need to come up with plans for your build as well as the location you plan on building. You can build anywhere as long as you own the property. Once you have your plans, show them to your local building department or building official.

As long as all your plans are in order, you should receive all the permits you need to build in your area. These permits include but are not limited to:

- A Building Permit

- A Plumbing Ppermit

- A Electrical Permit

- A Grading Permit

- A Discretionary Permit

Once you have all your permits in place, you can get started.

BOOK 9

Step 2: Choose your location

Choosing the location of your bunker is more than just building in a place you like. When considering your bunker location, think of a place that is secure and provides a moderate amount of privacy.

You'll want to avoid any areas that are near a large body of water, like a lake or a river, or your bunker is at risk of flooding. Avoid areas filled with trees or you'll have a web of roots to cut through while digging through dirt for your bunker. Stay clear of utility lines in the area. You'll want to stay at least 18 to 24" away from any utility lines in your area while digging.

Step 3: Design a Blueprint

Just like when building a house, you need to design a blueprint before getting started. Your bunker doesn't need to be large or have multiple rooms. It just needs to have a few necessities such as a bathroom, cooking area, and storage space.

You can make your build simple by combining areas in an open-floor plan. Utilize vertical space so you don't need as much horizontal space. Plan for wall mounted furniture to save on space. Keep your design a simple shape, like a square or rectangle. Plan for everything you might need so that nothing is left out until the end of your construction process.

Step 4: Choose your building materials

There are several choices when it comes to building materials, but you'll want to go with an option that won't crumble easily underground and will last for a long time. For instance, untreated wood will rot easily when used to build underground. Of all the options, the three best ones are:

1. **Bricks**

These are a sturdy and affordable option. They make great insulators and are weatherproof, which means they'll last longer before breaking down underground.

2. **Metal sheeting**

Metal sheeting is both sturdy and water-resistant, but it isn't the most cost effective option. Extra insulation will need to be added since metal sheeting provides poor insulation.

3. Concrete

Concrete is difficult to work with, but it is the best option when it comes to cost, durability, insulation, and lifespan. Reinforced concrete can last up to 200 years before breaking down.

These are the best options if you're picking a building material for building your own, personalized underground bunker. Keep in mind there are other options, but these either don't last very long, aren't strong, or don't provide much room for personalization.

Step 5: Gather key living materials

Building a structure in the ground and stockpiling it with food and water is good, but it's not enough. There are key ingredients to any sustainable form of life, and you need to make sure you have them.

1. Water filters

This ensures that a drinkable source of water is on hand at all times. Any water filter will do and you can even make your own.

2. A waste removal system

If waste is mismanaged, it can be dangerous for your health. There are several ways to manage your waste and keep your living area safe and sanitary. A composting toilet is the best option for off-grid living.

3. Ventilation and air filters

This will filter the air from outside and make sure it is clean and safe to breathe by the time it enters your bunker. An air filter is your best option when it comes to protecting yourself from air contaminants.

4. A generator or another form of off-grid electricity

Step 6: Reinforce your shelter

Reinforcing your shelter is a must, no matter how deep you intend on digging. When building an underground shelter, you can expect quite a bit of weight and pressure from the top pressing down on your bunker's roof.

Your shelter will need a proper foundation. Concrete is the best option for a solid foundation, but make sure you use reinforced concrete to lessen the risk of cracking or breaking.

Use metal beams to lift up the roof of your bunker and support it from collapsing. The walls of your bunker should also be at least 1 to 3 feet thick to add extra support.

Building an underground bunker can be as simple or as complicated as you wish to make it. If you find it difficult, you can even hire some builders and contractors to do the work for you. Remember that an underground bunker is only one of several underground shelter options.

Underground Shipping Container

This is by far the cheapest and simplest way to build an underground shelter. The shelter will already be built; all you have to do is reinforce the area and bury it.

Shipping containers are flimsy, so they can't be buried in the dirt straight away. The area needs to be reinforced and the shipping container needs to be added after the fact.

Step 1: Source a large shipping container

Most shipping containers are around 20 feet long, but there are larger ones. Depending on the size of your family, you may need to find a larger container. Source out the container that is right for you. You'll be using special tricks to make the most of your space, but buying large is still your best option.

Step 2: Pick a location

When it comes to building a shelter out of a shipping container, putting it straight into the ground isn't the best idea. The walls of a shipping container are flimsy and will bend easy under pressure.

The best location for a shipping container shelter is on the side of a hill. You can think of it as a cave with metal walls.

Step 3: Reinforce the area

Once you've found the perfect area for your shipping container shelter, dig out a hole that's slightly larger than your shipping container. Now reinforce the area by creating a foundation out of reinforced concrete.

Create a thin layer of concrete all around the area that you've dug out. The floor, roof, and walls should be covered in concrete. This creates a barrier around your shipping container so that the weight of the dirt doesn't bend the metal walls. The concrete also adds insulation.

Step 4: Modify the shipping container

A shipping container by itself doesn't make a good shelter. The shipping container needs some modification before you can safely call it a home. Holes for ventilation need to be cut and air filters need to be installed. An area for the bathroom needs to be separated from the rest of the shipping container. Holes for waste and air need to be drilled.

The shipping container itself needs to be waterproofed as well. You can do this by lining the outside of the container, aside from the ventilation holes, with plastic sheeting. Be careful with the plastic sheeting so you don't puncture or cut it.

Once you've done that, the only thing left to do is add plumbing options for a kitchen and shower area. If you would rather save on the space, you can build a separate outdoor shower near your shelter.

Step 5: Place the shipping container in the hill

Place your shipping container in the hole you've made for it. If there are any gaps, don't fill them because you need room for air. The front of the shipping container should be sticking out of the hill. Now you can use concrete to create a 'door' around the front of the shelter.

Remove the doors of the shipping container and leave the front open. Create a sort of dome around the entrance using concrete, leaving enough space in the middle to attach the doors from the shipping containers. Make sure you connect the concrete from the dome directly to the face of the hill and add a layer of plastic sheeting for waterproofing.

Step 6: Personalize

Most people don't like using the shipping container method because it doesn't allow for a lot of personalization. However, if you're smart with the space you use, you can personalize it to your heart's content.

Be sure to use foldable and wall mounted furniture. Think about how life would be if you lived in an R.V. Use up as much vertical space as possible and try not to clutter with any unnecessary comforts or belongings. Life in a shipping container can be tough, and it requires a lot of adjustment, but an experienced prepper knows that you can and will do anything in order to survive.

Temporary Shelters

Going into a preplanned and prebuilt shelter isn't always going to be an option. You could be thrown from your home unexpectedly or caught out in the wilderness in the middle of an emergency. When that happens, you need to be able to improvise.

Temporary shelters are things that we can make out of what we have around us or on us at the time. Knowing how to make a shelter on the go can save your life.

Round Lodge

A round lodge is a hybrid formed from many different cultures. If you want to picture it in your mind, think of a sweat lodge from the Native American culture. This shelter is quick and simple to make, but it requires the use of tools and some physical labor.

To build a round lodge, you need:

- **An ax or hand saw**

- **A large pile of dried grass or leaves**

Step 1: Cut some logs

You'll need to cut several thin logs using the ax or hand saw. You need enough to make a large, round structure.

Once you have enough logs, place them in the ground, leaning them up against each other at one end and burying them in the dirt on the other. You want to make a triangle shape at first and then round it as you add more logs, until it becomes a pyramid with a large space in the center and an open hole at the top.

Leave an open space at the front of the lodge for use as an entrance.

Step 2: Cover the structure

BOOK 9

The round lodge, once formed, provides a simple shelter, but it is still open to the elements. Covering the outside of the shelter with a thin layer of dried grass or leaves can help protect you from rain, wind, and the sun.

The hole in the center of the logs creates a space for smoke to escape, so if it's cold one night, don't be afraid to build a fire in your shelter.

Step 3: Add a door

Cut several more thin logs for the entrance. Make these ones shorter since you're only using them to cover up the top half of the entrance. Once that's done, you can use a tarp to cover the entrance, or you can make your own door.

To make a door, you'll need a few more thin logs, or long sticks, and some twine. Rope the sticks together until you've made a panel large enough to place over the entrance to the lodge.

Step 4: Cover the floor

You're almost done creating your temporary shelter. Now you need to cover the floor with dried grass or leaves in order to protect yourself from the cold. It's most likely you're building this shelter on a dirt floor, and a dirt floor can get very cold and damp at night. This makes it unsafe for use as a shelter. A simple covering of leaves or grass can save you from this.

The Leaf Hut

The leaf hut is similar to the round lodge, but works on a smaller scale. It's a two-sided, wedge-shaped structure. It's like a lean-to, but it's better insulated and weatherproofed by the layer of leaves covering it.

To build this shelter, you'll need:

- **A 9 to 12 feet long pole**

- **Several tree branches (with leaves)**

Take the long pole and place one end in the ground, digging it in for stability, and prop the other end up in the fork of a tree or set it on a stump. You need something stable to hold it up so it doesn't fall.

Lean the branches up against the pole, forming ribs for the structure. Place them at an angle along both sides of the pole until every opening is covered by the leaves still attached to the branches. Make sure to place the branches as close together as possible.

Next, cover the whole structure with some loose vegetation such as moss, grass, ferns, brush, or pine boughs. This will trap in the warm air and protect against the elements. Finally, throw some of the vegetation into the shelter for your bed. You can also throw some sticks or twigs on top of the shelter to weigh down the vegetation against the wind.

OFF-GRID LIVING

  Book 10

Book 10:

Life Without Electricity

We've all gone a day or less without electricity. We've all experienced a power outage, leaving us without our technology that we so desperately rely on. Humans managed to survive thousands of years before electricity, and yet we've become dependent on it. Society is at the point where completing simple tasks is impossible without electricity.

If you plan on living off-grid then you may have to come to terms with the fact that you won't have access to electricity. There are a few options for making your own power in an off-grid situation, but these are difficult, unreliable, and expensive at times.

However, with the world's pollution rising and our carbon footprint growing, the notion of off-grid living and surviving without electricity is growing in popularity. There are more and more people opting for a powerless life, and this is making it more obtainable and affordable for others who are truly committed to the idea.

If you are planning on going off the grid completely and leaving a life with electricity behind, you might be wondering how having no electricity will actually affect your life.

1. No clean, running water.

Modern water systems rely on electricity to manage systems and pumps that filter out water and make it safe. Without electricity, the water running through your tap is no longer safe and free of bacteria.

2. No central heating.

Winter months are made even harder without access to electricity. All modern central heating systems rely on electricity to function. Without it, we're forced to use old, simpler ways to keep warm during the winter.

3. No lights.

You won't realize how much you use your lights until they're taken away from you. Without electricity, your lights won't turn on anymore, and even flashlights won't work forever. Old methods of lighting, like using candles, will become when there is no electricity.

4. No cooking.

We rely on our stoves and ovens in order to cook our meals. We even use microwaves to heat up already prepared food. Without this, old slower methods of cooking will have to suffice.

5. No fridge or freezer.

Food won't last as long without electricity. We rely on our refrigerators and freezers to preserve our food and keep it fresh longer. Without this, we would have to get used to keeping food that doesn't need to be kept cold in order to avoid wasting.

6. No entertainment.

Most modern forms of entertainment rely on electricity, whether it's watching the television, listening to music on the radio, or playing games on our computers. All forms of entertainment rely on electricity.

7. No communication.

As with entertainment, all modern forms of communication rely on electricity. We use social media, WiFi, and our electronic devices to communicate and keep in touch with the outside world. Without electricity, all these things are rendered useless.

How to Live Without Electricity

Going off-grid and deciding to leave a life of comfort and convenience behind means living without electricity. The question isn't 'Can you do it?' The real question you should be asking is 'How can I do it?'

When considering life without electricity, there are only a few important things it will affect:

- **Water**

- **Food**

- **Heating**

- **Light**

- **Communication**

- **Entertainment**

If you're able to adapt and live without these things being provided easily through electricity, then you can survive in a world without electricity. Clearly, it's impossible to live without these things completely, so finding alternatives or replacements is a must.

Lighting

When it comes to lighting, if there is no electricity then there are little alternatives or replacements. Flashlights are usually the first thing people think of when it comes to alternative lighting, but for a long term solution, it just won't do.

Candles are very effective, long lasting, and cheap. You can buy them in bulk and store them since they never go off. Candles provide a moderate amount of light, but when complete darkness is the only other choice then the light they provide is more than good enough.

Oil lamps provide much brighter light than candles do, but they require you to have access to oil for fuel. A single oil lamp is bright enough to light up a whole room, but it uses about 2 cups of oil a night. As long as oil is available then an oil lamp is a great alternative for light, but it adds the risk of a fire hazard.

Solar powered lamps are bright, lightweight, and easily portable, but they are also expensive, and take a full day or more of bright, direct sunlight to fully charge. A solar powered lamp can be a good alternative since it poses less risk than an oil lamp and is brighter than a candle.

OUTDOOR SOLAR LAMP

Cooking

Cooking without electricity isn't a difficult as you might think. There are multiple choices, from old school options to more modern alternatives.

Ever since humans started cooking their food, they used fire, so this is an obvious alternative to using a stove or oven. Building a fire is easy, if you have the right tools and methods, but it poses a fire risk and can't really be done while indoors unless you have a fireplace.

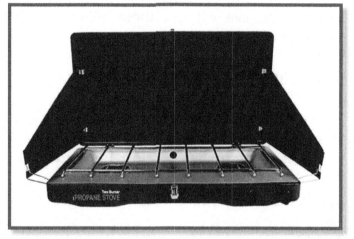

A more modern version of cooking without electricity involves using a propane gas stove. These are expensive, but will make you feel like you still have electricity. Unlike other cooking alternatives, a propane gas stove doesn't pose a risk or hazard, as long as it's used correctly and taken care of.

PROPANE GAS STOVE

Water

Most of the water provided by your city relies on electricity to clean and pump it, so without it, you won't have any clean or running water.

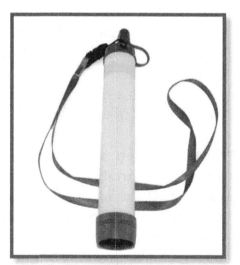

Alternatives include finding a nearby source of fresh water, stockpiling on bottled water from a store, boiling your tap water and storing it, buying or building a water filter, or catch rainwater and storing it.

A rainwater harvesting system is the most effective replacement and long term solution. As long as your area doesn't enter a drought, you should always have access to rain water. This is provided that the rain water doesn't become con-

WATER FILTER

taminated in the future due to high levels of pollution. If that is the case, then filtering and boiling water is the only option you have left.

Heating

Heating isn't always an issue. It can only become a problem during the winter months or if you live in a generally cold area. However, there are many alternatives to heating systems run by electricity.

Adding a fireplace to your home is a quick and easy solution to your heating problems. If you build your fireplace in the center of your house and add ventilation leading to all the rooms throughout the house, you can easily heat up your whole house without the use of electricity.

If adding a fireplace isn't an option, then traditional methods like bundling up, drinking a hot beverage, and wrapping yourself in a blanket are always going to work.

Preserving Food

Our refrigerators and freezers do so much work for us, but we won't realize how much we rely on them until they're gone. The modern human's diet consists of a lot of meat and perishables, meaning that losing the ability to freeze or refrigerate our food is a huge problem.

There are some refrigerators that run on propane, and there are also battery operated ones that can be charged using a car battery or solar power. However, the easiest and cheapest way to solve this problem is simply limiting the amount of perishable foods that we eat.

Foods with long shelf lives are a must in this situation, and learning how to preserve food without a refrigerator by rubbing it with salt or canning it is a must. A more extreme move you can make is running your own garden and raising your own animals to ensure that you always have access to fresh food.

Entertainment

It may not seem as important as having clean, running water, lighting, or fresh food, but entertainment is something that we need. If we go from living in a world where we're always kept busy and we're always entertained to a lifeless, boring world, then we'd start to slowly lose our minds.

Keeping entertained helps keep us mentally and physically active in some ways. It helps us relax and unwind, so life without it can be difficult. Luckily, there are plenty of ways to keep yourself entertained even without access to a television or phone.

Developing hobbies is the best way to keep yourself entertained. Learn to play an instrument, pick up a form of art, build something, or simply read a book. It may seem obvious, but you don't need electricity in order to have fun.

Communication

Being able to communicate with the world around you is important for multiple reasons. When humans are alone for too long, it starts to mentally affect them. We need social interaction to keep our minds functioning the way they're supposed to. Communication is also a number one source of information. We learn everything we know from other people, and being cut off entirely means losing that source of information.

Unfortunately, short of seeing people in person, there aren't a lot of options when it comes to replacing modern day technology.

However, if you don't have electricity but cell towers are still operational, you can get a solar powered charger for your phone and still use it to communicate with phone calls and text messages.

If not, then you can invest in a Citizens Band (CB) radio. These provide short range communication and need batteries to operate, but as an alternative to modern day communication, it's the best option available.

SOLAR RADIO

OFF-GRID LIVING

  **Book 11**

Book 11:

Methods of Composting

Plants are very much like humans, needing the basics of things to survive. Plants need water, energy, air, and food. In order to get food, plants use the energy they get from the sun to break down the nutrients in the soil. The more nutrient rich the soil, the better the plant will eat.

Composting is a controlled decomposition of green and brown organic materials. In compost, what we call green organic materials includes things like food scraps, grass clippings, and anything that is somewhat fresh and contains a lot of

nitrogen. Brown materials include things like wood chips, branches, dry leaves, and anything that is dead and contains a lot of carbon. These are the two ingredients you need to make a successful compost.

Compost acts as food for plants that helps them grow faster and stronger. Compost adds nutrients into soil that can help plants combat diseases and produce larger yields. There are many methods of composting, some being easier than others and others being more effective. The type of composting you do really depends on how much time you have to wait and what you have available to you.

Composting Basics

Before we get into the different methods of composting, let's start with the basics. It's not as simple as throwing all the ingredients together and waiting for the decomposition to start. There is a balance and an order to things. Follow the steps correctly and you can end up with a great batch of powerful, nutrient rich compost.

Particle Size Matters

There are a few things you need for a compost to be effective, one of them being microorganisms. The materials in compost only break down and start to decompose due to the microorganisms that feed on the materials. This is where size matters. By reducing the particle size of your compost ingredients, you create a larger surface area on which the microorganisms can feed. This makes their job of decomposing a lot easier.

Grind, shred, cut, and tear apart your ingredients before tossing them in to decompose. Creating smaller particles also improves the insulation in the compost pile, which in turn helps regulate the temperature of the pile. However, making the particles too small can disrupt the airflow and slow down decomposing. A perfect balance must be achieved.

Oxygen Flow

Aeration and airflow are important factors in a composting pile. The airflow is needed to oxygenate the materials and help break them down, making it easier

for the microorganisms to eat away at the food and decompose faster. Along with air, the compost also needs moisture, so great care must be taken not to add too much air to the compost or this could dry out the materials and stop the decomposing process.

There are many ways you can safely add airflow to your compost. Turning it regularly, as if you're mixing a bowl of food to get all the lumps out, helps. Another method is to add more things to bulk it up, like shredded newspaper, woodchips, and branches. This makes the compost less dense and allows for more airflow.

Moisture Content

The microorganisms living in your compost require a certain amount of moisture in the mix in order to survive. If the compost is too dry then your microorganisms will die out, which means nothing will break down your compost.

The green materials you add to the compost usually add their own moisture in varying amounts, but you can add extra moisture through intentional watering or waiting for rainfall. Careful not to add too much water, as this can drown your microorganisms and slow the process.

Temperature

Temperature regulation is the most important part of the decomposing process. Microorganisms need to live within a certain temperature range to produce the best results. A certain temperature can promote rapid decomposition as well as protect the compost from pathogens and weeds by destroying them.

However, controlling the temperature of your pile is the easiest step to take. As long as you maintain control of the other four factors mentioned above, you can control the temperature of your compost. When the microorganisms are healthy and active, the temperature of the compost's core should rise to at least 140 degrees Fahrenheit. This is the perfect temperature and can be maintained by controlling moisture, airflow, particle size, and nutrient balance.

Compost Materials

Understanding what compost consists of is a useful skill if you want to create

your own successful compost pile. There are only two ingredients when it comes to compost, brown materials and green materials. These make up the entirety of the compost, so their correct measurements are a vital step.

Brown materials, also known as dry materials, are usually carbon rich garden scraps. The brown materials give energy to the microorganisms and give body to the compost. Typically, brown items from your garden are used for this. They tend to be fibrous and wood-based in nature such as branches, sawdust, dry leaves, wood ash, shredded newspaper, tree bark, and much more.

Green materials, also known as wet materials, tend to be nitrogen based organic kitchen scrap. The green materials give the pile the proteins and amino acids that it needs for bacteria and fungi to function in the compost. Green materials are often organic waste from your kitchen such as egg shells, used tea bags, coffee grounds, banana peels, and other food scraps.

However, it can also include things like grass clippings and green leaves. Anything organic that is rich in nitrogen can be used as a green material.

While composting, you never want to use materials like meat, dairy, glossy paper, peanut butter, diseased plant materials, oily food, manure from carnivores, or ashes from a charcoal fire. These materials can kill the microorganisms in the compost pile and bring disease and rot with them.

As a general rule of thumb when composting, always use 2/3 of brown materials and 1/3 of green materials approximately. The measurements can change depending on whether or not you feel the pile is too wet or too dry.

Open Air Composting

The simplest way to start composting is with an open air method, which is the easiest method for beginners. This method involves simply creating a pile in your yard, or an open container, and tending to it only when necessary. It needs to be in a dry, shady area that is close to a water source and only needs a moderate amount of work and attention to be successful.

Let's get started:

1. Clear a space.

Find a spot in your garden that is out of the way, in the shade, near a water sour-ce, and clear it out. You want to remove any vegetation until you have a spot that is just bare soil.

2. Build a base.

Your compost pile is going to need drainage and airflow, so you can't just start piling it up on the floor. Build a base, a few inches tall, out of twigs or straw.

3. Add layers.

You can start adding layers of materials to the pile, one by one. Alternate betwe-en brown and green materials, waiting for each layer to start the composting process before adding the next layer.

4. Keep it moist.

The materials in your compost pile need to feel like a damp sponge. You don't want it to be too dry or too wet. When you touch the compost, you need to be able to feel that it is wet, but you shouldn't be able to squeeze water out of it if you grabbed a handful. If it feels too dry, add some water or green material. If it feels too wet then add some more brown material and stop watering it for a while.

5. Turn the pile.

Once you have the ingredients added, the only thing left to do is turn the pile once every few weeks. This allows the center of the pile to aerate and heat up. The aeration provides the microorganisms with oxygen and helps to regulate the temperature and moisture content of the compost.

That's it! You have your first open air compost. It's a simple method, but effective. Once your compost is ready, you can start adding it to your soil in order to help your plants grow large and healthy.

Direct Composting

Also known as trench composting, direct composting is a method used by new and inexperienced gardeners that prefer not to wait for a compost pile or even spend the time building one. Not everyone has the time or energy to spend on making a traditional compost pile, and for that reason, methods such as direct composting often work just as well.

Let's begin:

1. Dig a hole.

Pick an empty spot in your garden or pick a spot nearby some plants you have growing and dig a hole. The hole needs to be at least 12" deep, but can be as wide as you want.

2. Mix in materials.

You can dump a mix of brown and green materials into the hole you've dug. Try to make the mixture as balanced as possible, and give it a bit of a stir so they're mixed together. Then cover the top of the hole with some of the dirt that you dug out of it.

3. Wait.

Your job is done, and all that's left to do is wait for the decomposition process to start. It should take as little as a month before your compost is ready and you can start planting directly where you buried your ingredients.

Direct composting is simple and effective. You aren't required to turn it or water it at all. Once you've put the ingredients in the ground, the soil enriching process begins. You don't even have to move the compost once it's done. You can start planting your garden directly where you mixed your compost ingredients into the soil.

Yes, direct composting seems like it has a lot of benefits, but there are some downsides too. Animals, from a dog, to a raccoon, and even a bear can dig up the compost that you've buried and ruin your garden in the process. This is the same if you have a compost pile, but with a compost pile, it's out in the open and your garden and plants aren't put at risk.

Another downside is not being able to dig up and move the compost as you choose. With direct compost, you usually use it where you make it. If you want to start planting somewhere else, then you need to start making another batch of compost in that area because you won't be able to move the batch you already made.

Compost Tumbler

A compost tumbler is a device you can use to make composting a much easier job. It's a drum or bin you can mix your materials in and rotate easily. The compost tumbler consists of a large barrel-shaped container that is usually mounted on an axis with a handle for easy turning. It tumbles the compost, speeding up the process and making your job hands free and easy.

Compost tumblers help create the ideal environment for compost to decompose faster and more efficiently. The tumbler helps to effectively turn and mix the compost easily, creating air pockets in the mixture. These air pockets provide plenty of oxygen for the microorganisms and help them do their job.

The tumbler also eliminates the unpleasant things that come with composting, including strong odors and garden pests.

Using a compost tumbler is simple and only requires a few extra steps to be taken. Before you can start mixing in your tumbler, you need to decide what type of tumbler you need. The difference between the types of compost tumblers are simply size and the number of chambers available.

Along with finding a tumbler that is durable and will last long, you need to find one that is sized to suit your needs. When determining the sixze you need, you have to look at the amount of food waste you produce, the amount of garden scraps you have available, the size of your garden, and the food needs of your family.

If you have a lot of food waste and garden scraps available, then you would need a larger tumbler to make more compost. However, if you don't need to or plan on having a large garden, then a smaller tumbler is better suited for you.

Another thing to consider is if you need a dual-chamber or a single-chamber compost tumbler. Most compost tumblers available are a dual-chamber, which means it has two separate chambers. This provides a continuous use of the compost. One chamber holds old, already decomposed compost, while the second chamber is used to add new ingredients to start a second batch of compost.

Again, your decision to get either a single-chamber or dual-chamber relies on how much compost you need and how much you can make. If you aren't using up or able to make a lot of compost at once, then a single-chamber is probably a good enough pick for you.

Once you've picked a compost tumbler that suits you, there are only a few extra steps to follow:

1.   Place your compost tumbler in the shade.

2.   Feed your compost tumbler a handful of materials every 1 to 2 days until the mixture is about 4" from the top of the barrel.

3.   Cut up your compost to make it easier.

4.   Add ingredients like grass clippings carefully, as they can create matting unless sprinkled evenly.

5.   Turn your compost tumbler every few days in order to aerate the mixture.

6.   It's not difficult to use a compost tumbler and come out with a successful batch of compost. The hardest part is usually picking the right tumbler to suit your needs. After that, it's all about paying attention and being patient.

OFF-GRID LIVING

  **Book 12**

Book 12:

Survival Gardening

A survival garden isn't like any other kind of garden. This type of garden is carefully designed to yield enough food for you and your family to be able to live off of. If a survival garden is planned out perfectly, you and your family won't need any other food to live off of.

A survival garden, despite the name, isn't just made so that you and your family can survive. It needs to provide more than enough food for you to thrive. Supplying food through a garden isn't enough. You also need to get specific with the type of food you grow in your survival garden.

Essential vitamins, carbohydrates, minerals, fats, and some medicinal plants as well can all be grown in your survival garden.

Gardening by itself is a complex skill to learn, but with the addition of working on a survival garden, it becomes even more complicated. To be successful at creating a survival garden, you need to think like a survivalist. You need to think as if there are no stores to buy food from and the only food that you will ever have available is the food that you grow in your garden. If you think like that, then you can achieve success.

The Basics

The best time to start a survival garden is now, and it's best to start with the basics. Even though a survival garden is meant to service the dietary needs of every member of your household, you can't start with a garden of that size straight away. By starting with the basics, that means starting small.

As your gardening skills increase, so can the size of your garden. If you are new to gardening in general, then everything is going to take practice. There are several skills you'll pick up along the way and develop through trial and error.

The first steps for any garden are:

- **Selecting seeds**

- **Planning the layout of your garden**

- **Composting**

- **Knowing when to harvest**

- **Preparing the soil**

If you are ever deterred by the amount of work and learning that's required of you to develop your survival garden, just think of the joy and pleasure you'll feel when you're able to provide wholesome and healthy food for you and your family.

  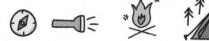

BOOK 12

The Best Survival Crops

The amount of space you have to work with and the type of climate you live in will greatly affect what crops you'll be able to grow. Know that if you plan out your garden correctly and plant the right seeds, you can grow your crops anywhere.

From a simple apartment garden to a large scale country garden, it only matters the type of seeds you decide to sow.

The type of crops you grow depends only on three factors:

1. Calories

It's recommended that every person, depending on their height, weight, and age, eat a certain amount of calories a day in order to function. Eat any less than what you need and you'll become shaky, sleepy, and weak or unenergetic overall.

Starchy and sugary crops are usually calorie-dense and should make up the bulk of your garden.

2. Nutrients

Calorie-dense foods usually lack nutrients, which also needed for a healthy and balanced diet. You can make up for the lack of nutrients by filling up the remainder of your garden with fruits, vegetables, and legumes. These will provide you with essential minerals, protein, and vitamins.

3. Storability

Growing all the food that you and your family needs means you'll have to properly store any food that isn't used straight away. Imagine a large crop of strawberries, ripe for the picking. Now imagine those strawberries 2 weeks later. Growing crops that store well is a make or break for a survival garden.

Keeping these factors in mind, and we can make a list of the perfect crops for a survival garden:

- POTATOES
- BEANS
- SQUASH
- CORN
- CABBAGE
- LENTILS
- KALE
- TOMATOES
- ONIONS

- SPINACH
- BEETS
- PEAS
- CARROTS
- PEPPERS
- HERBS

BOOK 12

Planning a Survival Garden

Planning your garden is just as essential as picking the seeds and buying them. You need to utilize every inch of soil that you have so that you don't end up with wasted space or not enough space. You don't want to plan out a garden and end up with too much food, but it's even worse to wind up with not enough food for your family. That's why the size of your garden is the most important thing to consider when planning your survival garden.

The size of your garden depends on several things:

1. How many family members you're feeding (since each family member needs to eat a certain amount of calories per a day).

2. The kind of crops you plan on growing (as some take up a lot more space than others).

3. Your experience with gardening.

4. The amount of free time you have to devote to your garden.

5. The amount of land you have available.

Depending on the size of your family and the land you have available, the maximum size of a survival garden for a regular family is around 2 acres. The minimum amount of land required for a smaller family is around ¼ acre.

It's best to start out small, and as each year goes by, you can grow your survival garden bigger to better suit your family's needs. The size of the garden doesn't necessarily affect the amount that each crop will yield. That fully depends on what crops you grow and how you plan out your garden.

Remember that your survival garden is a lot more than just a garden. It is your lifeline in a world where you have to rely on your own abilities to provide for your family.

OFF-GRID

SURVIVAL

Bonus Video Courses

To view the Prepper's Survival Bible video courses, go here:
https://www.youtube.com/@survivalistprepper

Introduction

Preppers try to prepare for the day when society falls apart and the way we live life today is gone. Even while we prepare for this, we still try to hold on to some of the comforts that come with modern life. We hold onto our homes, our conveniences, and the small things that make life easier. However, we must also plan for the day that we lose all of that and are left with nothing but the wilderness.

Whether you're stuck out in the wilderness only temporarily or you're forced to live out there, knowing how to survive is the key.

Humans require only 3 things in order to survive any situation, and that's why it's important to memorize the survival rule of 3:

1. **You can survive for 3 weeks without food.**

2. **You can survive for 3 days without water.**

3. **You can survive for 3 hours without shelter.**

The survival rule of 3 is not the only rule that you need to survive in the wild, but it is the most important rule that you will ever follow.

The main point of this rule is that when you find yourself out in the wilderness, you have to focus on your immediate problems first. You can't start panicking about things that don't directly affect you at the moment. When you're trying to survive, you can't think about the future. You have to live in the now.

The first and most immediate danger is shelter, because, depending on the temperature and wether, you can only survive about 3 hours in the extreme elements without shelter. Next is water, because our bodies need water within 3 days before it becomes a problem. After that the problem becomes food, since

  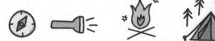

our bodies can survive a whole 3 weeks without food as long as we have water and shelter. As long as you know how to act an what to act on first, you'll find surviving out in the wilderness isn't impossible, it's just challenging.

Here are a few more rules of thumb when surviving in the wilderness:

1. **Tools are your best friends.**

Whether you bring a tool with you to the wilderness or you make one by sharpening sticks or grinding down rocks, a tool is going to be your best friend. Even a simple pocket knife can accomplish so much out in the wild.

2. **Stay in the area you know.**

After building your shelter and exploring the immediate area, it's not a good idea to wander around. The wilderness is tricky, and it's easy to lose your shelter and get turned around. If you're going to explore, do it slowly and always keep your shelter in sight or leave behind a trail you can easily follow.

3. **Most animals will avoid conflict.**

Aside from the elements, animals are your worst enemy out in the wilderness. Wild animals can be unpredictable and troublesome. However, a good rule of thumb is that animals want to avoid conflict. As long as you're not in an animal's territory and they aren't hunting you down for lunch, they'll want to avoid you, so you should take steps to avoid them.

4. **Sleep.**

It's scary out there and you might find yourself too frightened to close your eyes. Don't duct tape your eyes open just so you can keep an eye out for dangers or problems. Your mind and body need sleep in order to function. To be safer, instead of sleeping for 8 hours straight as we are used to, sleep in short intervals of 2 or 3 hours. Give your body the sleep it needs while still staying safe.

5. **Eat and drink as you need to.**

You may be wanting to save on your supplies and make them last longer, but don't skimp when it comes to meal times. Your body needs a certain amount of food and water to function. Don't hold back on what your body needs because you're afraid you're going to run out. Don't go overboard, and by all means ration your food, but don't starve yourself in order to do so.

6. Fire is your friend.

Fire is your new best friend. It keeps you warm, it gives you a place to cook or heat up your food, it can be used to boil contaminated water and make it safe to drink, it provides light in the dark, and it can even scare off some of the more unwanted animals you might run into.

With these rules as your arsenal and the willingness to learn from every experience, there's nothing that can stop you from not only surviving, but thriving out in the wilderness.

OFF-GRID SURVIVAL

  *Book 13*

Book 13:

Waste Management

An experienced prepper knows that your waste shouldn't just go to waste. There is a use for everything, even your waste.

Managing your waste, whether it's bodily waste, used water, or food scraps, is a huge step to really thriving in an off-grid environment. If you aren't willing to do the work and reuse your waste then that's all it is, a waste.

Compost Toilet

It might be hard to believe, but a toilet that flushes all of our waste away, never to be thought of again, is simply a luxury. It is a luxury that we cannot afford anymore. Many who see the damage that our water wasting ways are doing to our environment have decided to transition to more reusable forms of waste management.

A composting toilet is just one of the ways you can save on water and make your waste a more useful byproduct. Composting toilets recycle nutrients inside human waste and makes it safe enough to use as fertilizer.

Compost toilets are the perfect option for off-grid use. They can be purchased and set up easily or, for the more inventive and self-reliant person, they can be made. There are 2 types of composting toilets, working in different ways to reach the same result.

1. **Self-contained composting toilets.**

With a self-contained system, the waste capture is enclosed beneath the bowl, within the toilet. This system is well suited for small spaces.

2. **Remote composting toilet.**

With a remote system, all the waste is taken from the toilet to a remote location or a central collection tank. The toilet is connected to a collection tank via pipes. It's best to have the tank directly below the toilet so there aren't any twists or turns in the piping.

The composting toilet only works if it can separate the liquid waste from the solid waste. Once the separation is complete, the solid waste is mixed with an absorbent material like sawdust and turned into compost. No matter which type of compost toilet you decide to go with, they all follow the same method and will consist of the same parts:

- **Compost chamber**

- **Agitator bar**

- **Fan and vent hose**

- **Flush door**

- **Spider handle**

- **Flush handle**

- **Liquid drain**

- **Liquid bottle with handle**

- **Mounting screw**

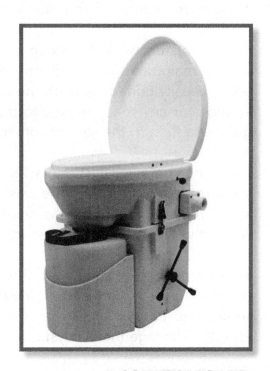

COMPOST TOILET

Along with these parts, you'll also need to line your compost chamber with carbon materials such as coconut fiber or dried peat moss. This is because the chamber needs to maintain a carbon/nitrogen balance in order for the bacteria to do its job.

The liquid waste is drained into a removable container and the solid waste is allowed to fall through a manual flush door. It is then delivered to the composting chamber. Then the spider handle, which is attached to the agitator bar, is used to stir up the compost.

Septic Systems and Greywater

Greywater is any runoff or waste water from the non-toilet plumbing systems in your home. This water comes from the basins, baths, showers, and washing machines. Greywater is usually wasted water, but if handled properly, it can be reused for your garden.

A septic tank is an underground system used to collect wastewater and treat it. With a septic tank in use, you can turn your greywater into safe water you can reuse in other areas of your home.

A septic system works by taking all the water from your house, which runs through one main drain pipe and into the septic tank. The tank is a watertight container usually buried beneath the ground. The tank holds the waste water long enough for any solids to sink to the bottom, becoming sludge, and all oil and grease to float to the top, becoming scum.

There are compartments and a T-shaped outlet that prevent any scum and sludge from leaving the tank. The wastewater, now free of solids and oil or grease, leaves the tank and enters the drainfield. The drainfield is usually a shallow excavation that is made in unsaturated soil.

Septic tanks can be purchased through many different suppliers. It's not recommended to set up your own septic tank as many things can go wrong, and if your septic tank leaks or floods, harmful water can be drained into the surrounding area and damage the ecosystem.

Tips for Using Greywater

There are two types of greywater; treated and untreated. Both have their uses, but caution must be taken, because if used incorrectly, greywater can be harmful to you and your family's health.

Treated greywater has less health risks and can be used for a wide range of household chores. However, greywater needs to be treated correctly, and all greywater treatment systems must have a certificate of approval. Proper greywater treatment systems are usually expensive to set up and also to operate. If done right, treated greywater can be used to water your garden, flush your toilet, and even do your laundry.

Untreated greywater has little to no uses in your household. During dry periods, untreated greywater can be used to water a garden, as long as no food that is going to be eaten is growing in that garden. If used incorrectly, untreated greywater can make you or your family ill.

Blackwater and greywater from your kitchen that is untreated should never be used. Blackwater is water that has come into contact with toilet waste, and when it is untreated, it becomes a huge health risk and should not be reused if not first properly treated.

General rules of thumb when it comes to reusing water are:

- Never reuse water that was used to wash family pets.

- Do not reuse water that has come into contact with the toilet or anything else attached to the toilet.

- Do not reuse water that comes from the kitchen sink or dishwasher.

- Following these few simple rules can ensure your family's health and safety while working with greywater and blackwater.

OFF-GRID SURVIVAL

  *Book 14*

Book 14:

Raising Animals in an Off-Grid Environment

Knowing how to raise animals in an off-grid environment is essential for becoming self-sufficient and independent. Relying on stockpiling long life food alone is not a long term solution for more severe emergencies or life changing events. If something is to happen, there is no way to know how long you'll be cut off from the world or how long it will take for society and the normal way of life to be rebuilt.

Raising your own animals provides a long term and self-sufficient method of feeding yourself and your family. Animals can provide you with fresh meat, milk, eggs, and other hard to obtain byproducts like cheese and butter. These are things that simply can't be stockpiled and might be hard to find an emergency situation. Animals can also multiply if kept properly, which means you can start with a small number of animals and end up with a large population that continuously provides for your family.

The Best Off-Grid Livestock

Choosing the right livestock for your off-grid home is essential. Not all animals are suited for an off-grid living situation. Some animals can provide you with useful byproducts, but are difficult to care for, especially in an off-grid situation. Other animals are simple to care for but don't provide any useful or essential products, making them a waste of resources, time, energy, and space.

This is why the choice you make in your livestock is the most important choice you will ever make.

Chickens

Chickens are the most common livestock kept in an off-grid living situation, and this is for a good reason. Chickens are really easy to care for. In fact, they practically care for themselves, needing only space to roam, a home to roost in, and some food to eat. Chickens also grow quickly, meaning you can start with a small number and very quickly find yourself with a large population. Chickens can provide you and your family with:

1. Eggs

The main reason for keeping chickens is because of the eggs they lay. Depending on the breed, most chickens will start laying eggs around 18 or 20 weeks old. They'll continue to lay eggs, which can be harvested for breakfast in the mornings. Introduce a rooster into the mix and the eggs hatch, meaning more chickens and more eggs.

2. Meat

Since chickens multiply quickly, they can also be used for fresh meat. When chickens reach a certain age, they stop laying eggs. These chickens can be used for meat instead. Meat is essential for a strong, healthy diet.

3. Gardening

Chickens make excellent gardeners. They till the soil when they scratch the ground and sand-bath, and their droppings make excellent fertilizer for vegetables or flowers.

4. Pest control

Chickens are natural pest repellent, especially if you're keeping a garden and having problems with insects. Chickens will eat almost any insect that could cause harm to your garden.

Raising chickens is simple, but it requires preparation. You need to have your backyard set up for your chickens before you introduce them to their new environment. Within 30 or 90 days, you can raise your chickens for both eggs and meat, but you should define which they will be. This is because different breeds of chicken are best for either laying eggs or being raised for their meat.

Proper preparation will guarantee success in raising your chickens.

If you are raising chickens from the egg or as hatchlings, you'll need a brooder. This is because your chickens will be taken away from their mother hen, which would usually provide them with warmth, water, food, and other things they would need. Without their other hen, you need to provide them with these things, and that's where the brooder comes in.

Eggs and newly hatched chickens need to stay in the brooder for a few weeks until they have developed all of their feathers. Once they have their feathers, they can keep themselves warm and they can be moved to your main chicken house or coop. This is where you'll put your chickens straight away if you get them at the point of lay.

The chicken coop is a vital part of raising chickens. They provide your chickens with shelter and security from the elements and predators. Your chicken coop needs to be big enough to house all your chickens without causing crowding. It needs to have a spot for each hen to nest. The coop must be waterproof, warm, and strong.

You can purchase a ready-made chicken coop, or you can make one by yourself. All you need is tools, materials, measurements, and a design. The size of your chicken coop will depend on the number of chickens you plan on keeping. You generally require around 3 square feet of space per chicken. So, design your chicken coop around the number of chickens you plan on keeping and add room to improve.

The floor of the chicken coop needs to be covered with a bedding made of sand, straw, wood shavings, old papers, or any similar material. The best option is to cover your chicken coop floor with a mixture of sawdust and wood shavings to absorb the chickens' droppings and help control ammonia. You should also provide your chickens with diatomaceous earth for their sun-bathing habits that help them dislodge parasites and mites from their feathers.

Beddings inside the coop need to be changed regularly, as well as the diato-

maceous earth. This is necessary to control the bacteria build up and odor in the coop. Most birds prefer to sleep on raised surfaces. Your chickens' bedding needs to be placed on roosting bars, which are wooden bars of different sizes mounted at different heights for your chickens to roost on. The different heights cater to different ages of chickens in your flock. Make sure the roosting bars are round and wooden, which is perfect for chickens to grip onto.

You'll need feeders and drinkers for your chickens as well. Chickens tend to feed off of the ground when they scavenge for their own food, so if you plan on providing them with food and water, you'll need feeders and drinkers. They should be slightly raised off the ground. Automatic feeders have rotating bars, which prevents the chickens from perching above the food or water, preventing any contamination from chicken droppings.

Rabbits

Rabbits are an easy and great addition to an off-grid environment. They are easy to raise and provide some simple but essential byproducts for you and your family.

1. Meat

Rabbits can be a great source of meat for you and your family when there is none to find. Rabbits provide healthy, lean, and easily digestible meat.

2. Fur

There are certain breeds of rabbits that have reliable pelts. These can be knitted into items of clothing and other useful household items.

3. Fertilizer

Rabbit droppings can be used as fertilizer for your garden straight off the ground.

Choosing the right breed of rabbit from the start will determine what reasons you raise your rabbits for. The rabbits you raise for meat generally won't be used for their pelts as well. Aside from that, caring for rabbits is a relatively simple job.

Rabbits mainly feed on greens, which means you can raise them on a tight budget. The best rabbit breed to raise for meat is the New Zealand breed. This is because of its resilience, making it easier for new breeders that are bound to make a couple of mistakes.

Before you begin, you need to decide if your rabbits are going to be raised indoors or outdoors. There are some breeders that prefer outdoor raising to indoor raising because it gives the rabbits a chance to get sunshine and fresh air. However, raising your rabbits outdoors exposes them to predators and illness. Indoor rabbits are kept safe from all that, but they do require a lot of space.

Rabbits that are kept outside need to have a pen to protect them from predators and they need to be given extra bedding to keep them warm at night and in cold weather. A rabbit's pen needs to be large enough to allow for free movement. Your rabbit should be able to easily stand up right, run around freely, and lie down.

Pens are for your rabbit's protection, but they should not be where your rabbit spends most of their time. There should be a large area where your rabbit can roam freely and have access to at all times. If you're keeping your rabbit outdoors, remember that rabbits are diggers. They will dig holes and they will even use these holes to escape their enclosure. Make sure the walls or fences around your enclosure go deep into the ground to prevent rabbits from burrowing under them. Regularly check the perimeter of your walls and fill in any holes you find.

Your rabbit requires a balanced and healthy diet of grass and oat hay or timothy hay. They should have a constant supply of hay and be fed an amount of grass every day. You can even give them small, low sugar vegetables as treats. Along with food, your rabbit needs fresh water every day. A heavy ceramic or metal water bowl is the best option for your rabbit. Do not use sipper bottles as these are unsuitable for rabbits.

An important piece of information about rabbits is that they are coprophagic. This means that they excrete two different kinds of droppings: cecotropes and fecal pellets. The fecal pellets are hard, round, dry waste. The cecotropes are soft, large, light-colored droppings. The rabbit's digestive system requires it to eat the cecotropes in order to absorb nutrients from food. So, when cleaning up your rabbit's pen and play area, be sure to take away the fecal pellets, but leave behind the cecotropes.

Clean your rabbit's area once every week, removing soiled bedding, cleaning water and food bowls, and spraying the areas down with vinegar. Spot cleaning should be done daily. Your rabbits also need lots of attention to stay happy and live long, productive lives.

Goats

Goats are a good choice for off-grid living due their small size. They are easy to care for, can be kept on a small piece of land, and will provide your family with many byproducts.

1. Milk

You can get milk from other livestock but dairy goats are the most manageable choice if you're new at keeping animals. If you choose the right breed, one goat can produce enough milk to feed your whole family.

2. Meat

Given their large size, when compared to chickens and rabbits, a goat can provide a lot of meat for you and your whole family. The meat from a single goat can last for months, so proper meat preservation techniques should be used.

3. Fiber

If you're raising goats for meat then you should also consider using their pelts. They're much larger than a rabbit's pelt and just as useful, especially during cold months.

4. Fertilizer

Goat manure can also be used as fertilizer for your crops.

Goats are simple to care for if you're an inexperienced homesteader, but they still require certain necessities.

Goats are grazers, which means they like to roam and nibble on grass or plants they find on the ground. This means that you'll need an adequate amount of space for raising your goats, but a large plot isn't necessarily required.

One adult goat can produce 90 quarts of milk for every month, but only for 10 months out of the year. The number of goats you keep must be dependent on how many family members you'll be providing for and how much space you have available. However, you should keep at least two goats to ensure that they don't get lonely. Never only have one goat. Goats can give birth to at least one baby a year, which means you can start with a small number at first and slowly grow your population when you feel you are ready.

BOOK 13

A goat also requires some form of shelter from the elements. A goat's shelter is simple. It just needs to be kept dry, clean, and draft free and your goats will be happy. For most climates, a three-sided shelter is perfect for goats, but make sure your shelter has a separate stall for housing sick or pregnant goats.

The floor of the shelter can be densely packed dirt, but you should cover it with a thick layer of straw, wood shavings, or the hay that your goats don't eat for bedding. Make sure to keep the bedding clean and dry in order to keep your goats happy and healthy.

You'll also need fencing around the area you're keeping your goats, since they tend to wander. Goats are escape artists, so your fence needs to be tall, sturdy, and secure. Goats will climb, knock over, and easily escape an inappropriate fence. If there is even a tiny hole in the fence, your goats will climb through it. If the gate latch on your fence is loose, a goat will use its lips to wiggle it until it comes free. They also chew on everything, including rope and electrical wire. A goat will even climb onto the roof of its shelter, so make the roof slanted and slippery to stop them from doing so.

A fence that stands at least 5 feet high with corners and gates braced from the outside can keep a goat in. Your fence can be made of stock panels, wooden fencing, a chain-link fence, or a mixture of a wooden rail fence with wire woven in. Keep an eye on your goats and make sure there's nothing near the fence they can climb onto, jump over, or chew on, and they won't be able to escape.

When it comes to feeding your goats, you can let them roam and graze for themselves. Meat goats do well if they are left to graze and given hay, but milk goats and pregnant goats require goat chow in their diets as well. If your goats are grazers, remember to rotate them to different areas so they graze evenly and don't foul up one area, which leads to a build up of parasites.

Sheep

Raising sheep can be very rewarding, even if you live on a small piece of land and don't think you have enough space. Sheep are extremely gentle and docile animals. They can also serve many purposes and provide in multiple ways for your family.

1. Milk

Some breeds of sheep can be raised to give milk. However, they provide less milk than cows or goats but are simpler to care for than the two.

2. Wool

Sheep develop a thick, lucious coat of wool over time. You can shear this wool off and use it for things like clothes, blankets, and so on. Sheep should be allowed to keep their wool over the winter, since this is when it will grow strong and thick in order to protect the sheep from the cold.

3. Meat

Sheep can also be raised as a good source of meat. Since they provide a lot of meat, some meat preservation techniques will be needed so you don't waste.

4. Fertilizer

Sheep's manure, like most large farm animals, is perfect for use as fertilizer for your crops.

Sheep are perfect for small homesteads, and are even seen as pets to some who keep them. They are relatively small when compared to cows, pigs, and horses. They don't need a perfect plot of pastured land since they're happy to graze on brush, weeds, and grass grown in poor soil. Sheep can also be trained to come when you call them, follow you around, and stand still when you order them to. Sheep also don't require a lot of space, and people have kept a small flock on as little as one acre.

Caring and feeding sheep is also a simple and easy task. They can be fed predominantly on grass and fresh hay. Salt can be added to their diet as a mineral and vitamin supplement. Along with fresh water, this makes up a healthy sheep diet. Hay should be placed in raised feeders, and sheep should be rotated around your property if they are grazing on grass. Sheep also require protein, so grain is a good thing to add to their diet if they are lacking in it.

Shelter and fencing is a must for sheep. However, they are less complicated to care for than goats in this instance. A simple, smooth electric wire or woven non-electric wire can make good fencing for sheep. In the summer or in hot climates, sheep need shade from the sun. This can be in the form of a tree or an open, roofed structure.

A sheep's shelter can be a simple three-sided shed that is facing the south. This should protect them from the worst of the elements. The size of the shed needs to allow for 15 to 20 square feet of space for each adult sheep. A small closed-off shed is needed for your sheep to give birth. Move the young sheep to this shed for more protection.

Training sheep is simple, and using food as a lure is the easiest method. Sheep will always move uphill and towards open areas, and sheep usually follow other sheep in the flock. Sheep will also always move away from things that frighten them. If you understand the way they move, then herding and handling them becomes an easier task.

Cows

Cows are the most difficult of any livestock to raise, especially on a small piece of land. Most cows are physically larger than any other livestock, which means they require more space. Cows are also bigger financial investment than any other livestock when it comes to both initial cost and maintenance. Cows are very useful when it comes to providing your family with both meat and milk. They produce the most milk and meat than any other livestock while keeping less of them.

BOOK 13

Knowing what you want to raise a cow for is the first and most important step. Dairy and meat cows need to be raised differently, which means, depending on which cows you decide to keep on your land, the way you design your infrastructure and land is solely dependent on the type of cow you plant to raise.

Raising cows solely for their milk can be a costly endeavor. Cows can only begin producing milk after they reach 2 years of age and have had their first baby. Yes, cows need to have a baby before they can start producing milk. Once a cow has a baby, it will continue to produce milk for two years until it runs dry. At that point, the cow needs to have another baby before it will start producing again.

A single cow can give you way more milk than you would ever consume, which means you'll be wasting milk at that point. Raising a cow solely for milk can be a waste of money, time, and energy. However, if you plan on raising cows for both milk and meat, it becomes a more worthwhile investment.

Cows can be difficult to process for meat. You need a specific set of skills and a specific facility made for processing cows. If you're able to do both then raising cows for both beat and milk is your game.

When doing both, you can raise a cow for milk, making sure it gives birth to a calf every two years or so, and then raise the calf for meat. Grass fed cows can be ready to be processed for meat in 28 to 30 months. Grain fed cows are ready in 15 to 16 months.

Since a cow produces so much milk, you won't need more than one milk cow. This means you don't have to raise any of her calves for anything other than meat. However, your milk cow will reach an age where she won't be able to give birth or produce milk anymore. So, keeping one of her calves and raising it to take her place when you're closing in on that time is a good idea.

The quality of the land you keep your cow on is very important. Cows require a large amount of space. You can get by with at least 1 acre per a cow, but more is recommended for happier cows. The quality of the soil and grass grown on it is also important. Unlike sheep, cows won't do well on poor grass grown in poor soil. The poorer the grass, the more of it they'll eat. If you don't have proper land with good quality grass, then supplementing their diet with grains and mineral supplements is the route to go.

Along with their food, cows need a large, fresh supply of water. Their water sources need to be cleaned and refilled every day to ensure the water is fresh and free of bacteria.

Fencing and shelter is essential for raising cows. Cows are strong, and can push over a poor fence just by leaning on it. Make sure your fences are sturdy and stuck deep in the ground.

Cows are hardy, but just like any other animal, they need shelter to help escape the harsh elements. A large barn that is water-proof, kept dry and clean, and sheltered from the wind is perfect for any cow.

Raising any animal is no easy task. It takes hard work, dedication, and time to properly raise livestock to provide for you and your family. If you are willing to learn and do what needs to be done then you can only be successful in your journey ahead.

OFF-GRID SURVIVAL

  *Book 15*

Book 15:

Trapping, Fishing, and Hunting

Preppers know that there will come a time where conventional ways of running to the store for food are going to be a thing of the past. There will be a day where the stores won't be open and there won't be any food on the shelf.

When you're living in an off-grid environment, learning how to catch your own food through trapping, fishing, and hunting is an essential skill that cannot be taken for granted. In survival situations, you cannot deny the fact that meat provides us with much needed calories and nutrients. You can't hope to survive on your garden alone.

Trapping and fishing are simple tasks, but hunting is a dangerous sport that requires training and knowledge. These are the many ways you can get meat while out in the wild, and wheterh you chose to be a hunter, a fisher, or a trapper, you are choosing a new way of life.

Trapping

In survival situations and off-grid environments, traps can be used to capture animals without the need for you to track them down through the woods and hunt them. Think of traps as little hunters. You set them up and go about your day while they do the work for you.

There are hundreds of different traps that can be used in survival situations; some are simple to set up and others are complex and elaborate. Traps, at their most basic, are designed to capture, choke, hang, crush, or entangle a wild animal. However, the best thing to know about trapping, aside from setting up the traps, is where to place them.

As a rule of thumb, the more traps you set, the more likely you are to catch an animal. However, the best way of making sure that all your traps are successful is to place them where there'll most likely be an animal passing by.

When looking for an ideal spot to place your trap, you'll want to keep an eye out for:

- Animal tracks and their droppings

- Feeding sites and watering holes

- Chewed vegetation

- Known runs and game trails

- Den holes and nesting sites

A good trap set up in a bad location is just a bad trap. It's important to learn the area and memorize where the animals in your area frequent. Then you'll find the perfect spots to place your traps.

Common Survival Traps

There are typically two types of traps; a snare and a deadfall. There are plenty of other traps, but the most used and easiest to set up traps are usually a combination or a variation of the snare or the deadfall trap. If you learn how to build these two types of traps then you'll be set for a life as a trapper.

The easiest and most successful trap for any inexperienced trapper is the snare trap. It can be made anywhere using many different materials.

Snare Trap

A snare is basically a small noose that hooks around an animal's neck and is triggered to snap upwards, hanging the animal. It's mostly used for small game like rabbits and squirrels. It's usually placed outside of a den hole or on a known animal trail.

To build the noose, you need a sturdy material. The best material is usually wire, like headphone wire, craft wire, an uncoiled spring, or stripped wires from cars. If you don't have wire, you can use cord or string like dental floss, shoelaces, and fishing line. If you can't get a hold of any of that then nature's tools can help. Use cattail, milkweed, or dogbane to substitute wire or string of any kind.

To set up your trap, you'll need a sapling (young tree) that is strong but is still bendy. It doesn't have to be too tall, but must be able to hold the game your trap catches high in the air, safe from other predators until you find it. If there are no saplings around, then a large tree limb and a rock is an alternative method with the same idea.

Now you need to make your hook. This can be carved out of two pieces of wo-o\d. The one piece needs to be long and carved into a stake on the one end. The other end needs to have a notch cut into it. This will be your base. The other piece of wood can be short with a piece sticking out at one end that will fit perfectly into the notch of the other piece. This will be your hook.

Drive the base into the ground near your sapling; the two will be working together to form the trap. Tie your wire, string, or other material around the top of the sapling with a strong knot. Remember that the animal will be struggling and you don't want the knot to come undone. Tie your hook to the other end of the wire.

Now, pull the wire down and attach the hook to the base until the wire is pulled tight and the top of the sapling is bending down. You want that tension. Think of how you would put your fingers together, interlocking with your nails pressing into the flesh, and pull your elbows apart. This is the type of tension you want to create.

When your hook is in place, the sapling should be bent at a 90 degree angle, so make sure your wire is the proper length for this to happen. When the hook is removed by the animal, the sapling should straighten, dangling the animal you've just caught.

The final step is to tie the noose. The noose needs to be attached to the bottom of the hook. This knot needs to be secure, and the noose needs to be wide enough for the animal's head to easily fit through. At this point, the hook should have two cords attached to it; one for the sapling and one for the noose.

Place the noose on the ground and spread it out so it's wide enough for your target to get caught. You can place some bait in the middle of the noose to entice your prey. You can cover up the noose with some small twigs or stones; these won't interfere with the trap when it's set off.

Your snare is set to catch some game, and all you have to do is wait and come back to check on it.

Fishing

You know the old saying, "Give a man a fish and he'll eat for a day, but teach a man to fish and he'll eat for a lifetime."

Fishing is a simple yet effective way to keep both you and your family fed in survival situations.

Humans have been fishing since the dawn of civilization. It's an ancient skill that has never faded from our history. With fish being such nutritius and tasty sources of protein, it's no wonder why so many of us have taken up fishing as a way of survival. In order to be a successful fisherman, you don't need to buy the fanciest fishing rod or use the best bait. You just need to know the small tricks and tips that many experienced fisherman use to help them catch enough fish to live off of.

The first tip is making sure a survival fishing rod is a part of your survival kit. If you don't have one or can't get one, then you can make one. All you need is a willow reed or strong stick to make the rod, and tie a fishing line or something similar to it. Don't just stop at making one; make several of them. A hook can be made by carving it out of a piece of wood or using an old paperclip. Once you have your fishing rod or fishing line, the rest is simple.

A Trotline

This is a passive way to catch fish if you have other things to do and can't give your fishing line your undivided attention. You'll need your fishing line, a narrow and shallow part of a creek or river, and some cover or shade.

Take a paracord, or something similar, and tie each end of it to a strong tree branch on either side of the water. This is called your control line. Now, take some fishing line and tie one end to the paracord so that the other end is dangling in the water. You can tie several lines along the length of the paracord. Tie a hook and add some bait to the end of your fishing line and leave it. When you come back, you should have caught one or more fish.

A Fish Net

In some survival situations, you might not have access to a fishing rod or fishing line. In this case, you can still catch fish using a fishing net. Fishing nets can be made out of multiple materials. The green wood inside sapling trees can be used as a makeshift fishing net, and even a piece of cloth tied to two sticks can be used instead.

All you have to do is wade through water slowly and towards the shore. When you get to the shore, make sure to lift your net up slowly and carefully so you don't tip your catch out and back into the water. The successfulness of this depends on the population of fish in the water you decide to wade through.

Spearfishing

Spearfishing works on larger fish because they tend to be slower. You can make a fishing spear by taking a long, sturdy piece of wood and sharpening the one end to a point. You can use a pocket knife for this if you have one. If you don't, then rubbing the wood against a rock until it's grinded down can also work. ou can also grind down a pebble until it's sharp and attach that to the wood with twin or rope of some kind.

When spearfishing, aiming correctly is the key. You have to compensate for the light refraction on the water. You can do this by aiming below the fishe before you strike. Spearfishing is best done at night while using a torch for a light. That way you won't cast any shadows on the water, which is what alerts the fish to your presence and scares them away.

In the end, there are plenty of ways to catch fish for you and your family to live

on. Even in a survival situation, you can become an expert fisherman and provide enough food to live off of in your new off-grid life.

Hunting

Preppers and hunters usually fall into separate categories, but in reality, they have more in common than you would expect. Each is preparing for a disaster that could be waiting for them right around the corner. A hunter learns to be good at what he does through other hunters they meet out in the field and from their own failures and successes. The same can be said for a prepper.

Since hunters and preppers have so much in common, it's not too much of a leap to see a prepper become a hunter in an off-grid or survival situation. There are several types of hunting, most of which require a weapon and stalking strategy of some kind. Knowing the different forms of hunting and practicing each one can mean success in your ventures.

Bow Hunting

Bow hunting is the preferred hunting method for those who want to stay in touch

with the more primal nature of the sport. Bow hunting is silent and stealthy. It allows for opportunities to grab more animals before going home, since there is no sound to alert any nearby animals to your presence.

Bows don't have the power that more traditional and modern hunting weapons have, so aiming true and being accurate is the most important skill in this type of hunting. It's difficult to aim at the smaller animals with a bow and actually hit the target. For this reason, most bowhunters generally go for larger game, like elk.

A bowhunter's tool kit includes a hunting knife, extra bowstring, extra arrows, extra arrowheads, and a rangefinder.

Rifle Hunting

Rifle hunting is as subtle as bow hunting, but it is far more powerful, and some hunters say it is even easier. Loading another bullet into a rifle is simpler than loading another arrow into a bow. The bullets hit harder as well. Rifle hunters can even target smaller game, as it's simpler to aim with the rifle than with the bow.

Along with all these benefits comes a few downsides. A rifle is very load. That means that if you take your shot but you don't hit it, it's likely that whatever animal you were aiming at has run off before you can take another shot. Not only have you lost the animal you were hunting knife, extra ammunition, and general camping and hiking gear. Larger rifles need to be used for larger game, like bears. Which means you might be carrying more than one rifle with you as well.

Tracking

Regardless of which weapon you choose to use, there are still other methods for hunting. Tracking requires extreme skill at reading the earth and figure out which direction the animal is heading. Bow hunters are more likely to take the tracking route than rifle hunters, due to the fact that a bow won't scare away the animal if a shot is missed. A rifle shot would scare an animal away to the point where it could be untraceable.

A skilled tracker can almost always find the game that they are hunting by recognizing its tracks, scat, and other signs that animals have been through an area. Tracking is a skill that is built over years. It can't be learned easily, but practice and patience is key to tracking down your hunt. A tracker will have little of anything in their pocket, since traveling lightweight makes it easier to follow close behind their hunt.

Decoys and Hides

Using decoys is a popular form of hunting for waterfowl, but decoys for larger game is not unheard of. A decoy is a plastic figure made to look like the animal you're hunting. It's placed in a spot where those animals frequent and used in conjunction with enticing scents or calls for the animal you are hunting. Hunters then hide within sight of the decoy and wait for the animal to come looking.

Hides are also used without decoys. Hides are usually camoflage sitting areas hung in trees or hidden in bushes. A hunter sits in the hide, which is placed near known game trails or watering holes, and waits. It's the simplest form of hunting because all it requires is patience and good aim when the animal finally arrives.

The main downside to this type of hunting is the setup time is long and the chance of success is low. You are fully relying on there actually being animals in the area and coming to where you can shoot them. There's no guarantee that the animal you are after will even make an appearance.

Hunting isn't everyone's sport, but it is a reliable source of food for you and your family if you have the patience and desire to learn and develop the skill. Knowledge and experience are the hunter's best and most cherished resources.

OFF-GRID SURVIVAL

  **Book 16**

Book 16:

Essential Tools

An off-grid survival lifestyle requires various tools for everyday tasks and jobs. These essential tools can make life a little easier for you, and you really can't have a successful off-grid home without them. These tools can be as simple as a screwdriver for repairing broken equipment to something more important like a scythe for harvesting crops.

Harvesting Tools

The word harvesting here can be applied to any object that can be used for extracting any resources that can be used for consumption by you and your family. That includes crops from your garden, food that can be foraged, wood for building campfires, and water that can be collected.

The following are harvesting tools you want in your arsenal when you start your off-grid life.

1. Buckets

This is a simple multipurpose tool that anyone should have, even if you're not in an off-grid situation. These can be used for collecting water, transporting compost, and storing things.

2. Short handled ax

An ax is the perfect tool in your toolbox. When living off-grid, you'll find yourself in need of wood for multiple reasons. The most notable reason being to build a fire during the colder months of the year. A short handled ax will make the task of chopping wood for all your needs easy to accomplish.

3. Cant hook

After chopping wood, you'll need to transport it. A cant hook is basically a long grabbing tool. While using them, it's easier and faster to haul wood around, and your back will thank you for it later.

4. Rotary tiller

Depending on the size of your garden, tilling the soil can be a long and laborious task. A rotary tiller can cut the work time in half and till your soil for you at a rapid speed. Making seed planting an easier and faster task to complete.

5. Gardening tool set

There are plenty of tool sets for gardening that come with a collection of trowels, shears, shovels, and so on. A good set can come with everything you'll need for gardening and last you a long time.

6. **Tarpaulin**

A tarpaulin has multiple uses. It can be used as a blanket, shelter, rainwater collector, dust-protector, and as a quick-drying barrier.

Tools for Repair

To be truly self-sufficient, you must be able to rely on yourself alone. That includes being able to fix things when they break and solve all of your problems by yourself. A toolbox filled with tools for repairing your homestead as it ages and eventually breaks down is essential for success in an off-grid environment.

1. **Duct tape**

If it can't be fixed with duct tape then it can't be fixed at all. Make sure you always have a roll available.

2. **Carpenter pencils**

A carpenter pencil can be used to mark cutlines on wood, posts, and boards.

You'll most likely need this to help with your repairs and DIY projects.

3. Tool set

A tool set is the same as a gardening tool set. If you purchase the right one, you'll have a collection of simple tools like a screwdriver, boxcutter, hand wrench, and so on.

Tools for Health and Safety

Living in an off-grid environment means you're far away from any help and any medical care. Aside from extreme emergencies, you should be able to take care of any minor injuries that can occur.

1. Tweezers

These are ideal for removing small pieces of glass, ingrown hairs, splinters, and other things that may get caught in your skin. They are also a multipurpose tool and can be used for things outside of health.

2. Antiseptic

Antiseptic helps clean open wounds and disinfect them. This can help to slow down the growth of infections or stop them from forming all together.

3. Soap

A good, old fashioned bar of soap can help wash bacteria away and break down the membranes of viruses. Soap can keep you safe and healthy if used to wash your hands regularly.

4. Earmuffs

Earmuffs can help protect your ears from noise pollution that can take its toll on your ears eventually.

5. Safety glasses

Your eyes are precious and you should never leave anything to chance when it comes to them. If you plan on doing any work that puts your eyes at risk of injury, then safety glasses should be worn at all times.

6. Fire extinguisher

It's better to have something and never use it than to not have something and end up needing it. In an off-grid situation, you never know when a fire might break out, and you can't expect a firetruck to come screaming down the driveway.

Tools for Everyday Life

Tools for use during your everyday life can make or break your off-grid living situation. You need to consider each of them and seriously think about how useful they can be. For instance, a pair of gloves might not be that necessary at first, but you'll soon find yourself needing a pair and kicking yourself for not adding one to your toolbox.

1. Walking boots

A proper pair of walking boots can last you up to ten years. The best ones are insulated against cold weather, chemical resistant, slip-resistant, made of sturdy material, and equipped with steel toes.

2. Work gloves

Wearing well-insulated, comfortable, and padded gloves can save your hands from blisters, aches, cuts, and splinters. If you find a good, long lasting pair, be sure to buy a lot of them.

3. Bicycle

In an off-grid environment, you can assume that you won't be able to use a car at at times. Bicycles make a great form of transportation. They are easy to fix if they break down, don't need gas or power to run, and if you add a basket on the back or front, you can use it to transport goods as well.

4. Shovels

You never know when you'll need to dig some holes or pull a bush out from its roots. Shovels of all kinds can be useful. Long-handled shovels, short-handed shovels, round shovels, and pointed tip shovels are all useful in their own ways.

5. A knife

A good knife is worth a thousand useful tools. A good, long pocket knife has a thousand uses and should be a common item found in everyone's pockets.

6. A compass

A compass is seen as a dead art, since GPS and phones with navigational systems are now the thing of the future. However, in an off-grid environment, you can't hope to rely on those things. A compass is a must-have along with either a map or a simple understanding of your surrounding areas.

7. Rope

Rope is a multipurpose tool and a must-have for any toolbox.

OFF-GRID SURVIVAL

  *Book 17*

Book 17:

Home Medicine and First Aid

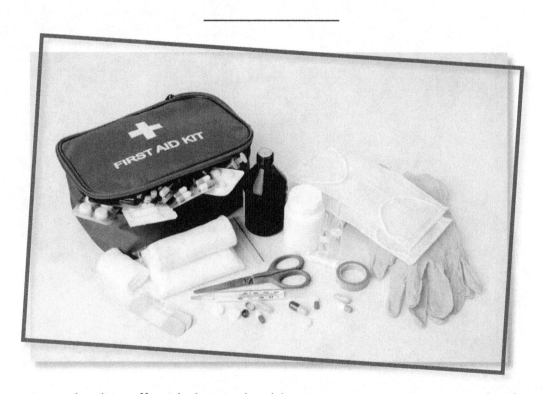

If you intend to live off-grid, then it should come as no surprise to you that knowing simple first aid and home medicines is a must. Accidents happen. It doesn't matter how careful you are, you or a family member can get hurt and there's no way to avoid that.

In an off-grid environment, help isn't going to be just around the corner. You won't have the option to call for help or rush to a hospital. In these instances, it's good to know how to deal with injuries and illnesses by yourself.

Survival First Aid Kit

A survival first aid kit is built with the intention of treating any minor serious injuries that may occur while living off-grid or in the wilderness. These injuries are usually not life threatening. Your first aid kit should be equipeed to deal with:

1. **Cuts (deep or shallow)**

2. **Stings or bites (from bugs or animals)**

3. **Burns**

4. **Abrasions**

5. **Strains**

6. **Splinters**

7. **Sprains**

8. **Fevers**

9. **Allergies**

10. **Aches and pains**

11. **Gastrointestinal problems**

12. **Sore throats and coughs**

You can equip your survival first aid kit to deal with even more serious injuries, such as breaks and extreme loss of blood. However, you should only have to worry about dealing with these injuries in extreme conditions. If conditions are not extreme then you should try your hardes to seek out professional medical assistance with these types of injuries.

BOOK 17

Your survival first aid kit should contain all or most of the following items:

1. Scissors

Used for cutting bandages to size, cutting through clothes to get to an injured area, and so on.

2. Adhesive tape

Used for sealing up wounds and taping down bandages.

3. Adhesive bandages (all sizes)

To be wrapped around large wounds or abrasions.

4. Plasters

Used for small cuts.

5. Tweezers

Used for safe removal of splinters, ticks, and stingers.

6. Gauze pads

These are sterile pads that can be used to clean and cover wounds, and can even be used as a soft, temporary eye patch.

7. Ace bandages

These can be used for wrapping sprained joints, wrapping around splints, or for wrapping a gauze pad onto a wound.

8. Latex gloves

A box for these can be used as protection against bacteria and infection while treating wounds. They can also be filled with water and used as an emergency ice pack.

9. Non-Adhesive pads

These can be used to cover wounds like burns.

10. Triangular bandage

This is useful for creating a sling and used as a towel or tarp.

11. Calamine lotion or Bactine spray

These are anesthetic treatments used for insect bites and itching rashes.

12. Diphenhydramine

This is an oral antihistamine used for allergic reactions. It's better to use this than cream when it comes to certain rashes.

13. Polysporin antibiotic cream

This can be applied to small wounds in order to combat infection.

14. Pocket mask

This is used to aid in CPR.

15. Safety pins (small and large)

These can be very useful securing a sling, non-adhesive bandages, and for removing splinters.

16. Burn cream and ice pack

These are for minor burns where only the top two layers of skin have been affected. Any lower and you may need professional help.

17. Non-prescription painkillers

These can be used to treat headaches, muscle pains, and so on.

18. Antibiotic ointment

This can be extremely helpful when it comes to treating cuts and open wounds as well as preventing them from getting infected.

19. Cotton balls and cotton swabs

These can be used for more precise cleaning of wounds, under the fingernails, ears, and eyes.

20. A list of every family member's allergies, medical history, and past injuries or illnesses.

These few things can help you keep your family safe and healthy by treating minor injuries. For more extreme and serious injuries, you may require the help of a medical professional.

Homemade Medicines and Remedies

Cultures around the world have been relying on their own traditional medicines and home remedies to treat their wounds and illnesses. For centuries, humans have been able to use nature and improvise rather than rely on medical advice and doctor prescribed medicine.

Preppers can use the same ideas and strategies when it comes to living off-grid. You can't pop down to the store whenever you need something to help your sleep or something for a headache.

Knowing some simple homemade medicines and remedies can help you not only survive, but thrive in an off-grid environment.

Medicinal Herbs

You can add these plants and herbs to your garden so you'll always have them available when you need them. Turn them into a powder or brew them into a tea; either way you can use these plants to help cure some minor medical problems.

1. Ginseng

The roots of this plant can be dried to make into powder or steeped in hot water to make tea. In traditional Chinese medicine, this plant has been used to boost immunity, reduce inflammation, and raise energy levels.

This herb is considered safe for short-term use but the safety of long-term use is unclear. Some side effects of long-term use include poor sleep, headaches, and digestive issues.

2. Echinacea

Commonly known as coneflower, this flowering plant is originally from North America. The Native Americans used it to treat a variety of things, including burns, sore throats, open wounds, toothaches, and upset stomachs. It has also been used to prevent or treat the common cold, but the science behind this is unclear.

Most parts of the plant can be used, including the leaves, stem, and petals, but people believe that the strongest effect comes from the roots. It can be brewed

into tea, which is the most common use, or it can be applied topically.

Short-term use is safe, but long-term use is not. Side effects of using this plant are stomach pain, skin rash, and nausea.

3. Elderberry

Elderberry is an old herbal remedy made from cooking the fruit of the Sambucus nigra plant. This remedy is used to treat nerve pain, colds, toothaches, headaches, viral infections, and constipation.

The unripe fruit is toxic and can cause vomiting, nausea, and diarrhea.

4. Ginger

Ginger can be eaten dried, fresh, or brewed into tea. It's long been used to treat

nausea, colds, high blood pressure, and migraines. Ginger is safe in low doses, but high doses can cause diarrhea and mild heartburn.

5. Turmeric

Turmeric is in the same herbal family as ginger, and it has been used for thousands of years in both cooking and medicine. Turmeric was first noticed for its anti-inflammatory properties. It can be used to treat a variety of ailments like anxiety, chronic inflammation, metabolic syndrome, and various pains.

Very high doses can cause side effects like skin irritation, headaches, and diarrhea.

6. Chamomile

Chamomile is a flowering plant that has been long used in teas and as a popular herbal medicine. Although the flower is used to make tea, the leaves can be dried and also used to brew tea.

Chamomile is used as a remedy for diarrhea, nausea, stomach pain, constipation, UTIs, upper respiratory infections, and open wounds. Chamomile is also believed to help with sleeplessness.

The only reaction you can get from chamomile is an allergic reaction, especially if you have known allergies towards small plants like marigolds and daisies.

Safety and caution must be taken into account when thinking about using herbal remedies. There are side effects, and long-term use is not advised. The quality of the herb and the soil it was grown in can also affect the use of the herbs. Most herbal medicines are not safe for consumption or use by pregnant or breastfeeding women and can be deadly if a pet or animal gets a hold of it.

The bottomline is, many people around the world have been using herbal remedies for centuries, but they can't replace modern medicine completely. Certain illnesses and ailments just can't be solved by herbal tea. Keep that in mind when you're thinking about treating yourself and your family. Sometimes you need help and there's no getting around that.

PREPPER'S
PANTRY

Introduction

The Prepper's pantry is a place where you'll always find what you need even during the worst situations. It's a place where you'll find food and water stored away safely and available for everyone who needs it.

An experienced prepper has many skills and much knowledge. Amongst that knowledge and talents hides the proper way to collect and store food and water.

In the situations where food and water is in short supply or not available at all. Stores are empty or closed. The water coming out of the taps is contaminated and unsafe. The only person you can rely on to find food and water that is safe for consumption is yourself.

The most important skill you can learn is how to properly collect and safely store food and water in your home for when you'll desperately need it.

PREPPER'S PANTRY

  **Book 18**

Book 18:

Water Sources and Storage

Water storage, water filtration, and water sourcing are skills that go hand in hand in survival situations. If you can't find clean water sources, then you need to know how to purify the water that you have available. If there isn't a lot of safe drinking water available, then you need to know how to properly store what you have so you can make it last.

Storing a proper amount of water per person in your household is the first step. You need at least 1 gallon of water a day for each person for both drinking and sanitiation. Pregnant women and sick people will generally use more water than that, and everyone will tend to need more water in hot climates.

It's recommended to store up to 2 weeks' supply of safe drinking water, if possible. However, you might need to store even more than this in certain situations. Water does have an expiry date, so you can't store water for too long. Most store-bought water bottles come with an expiry date that you can go off of. Non-store-bought water should be replaced after 6 months as a general rule of safety.

When you can't store enough water for a long enough time, you need to rely on finding safe drinking water sources or learning how to purify unsafe drinking water.

Water Sources

Finding safe drinking water sources in your home or in your area can mean the difference between life or death in a survival situation. There are many sources of safe drinking water both inside and outside your home. You just need to know where to look and how to spot them.

Water Sources Within Your Home

1. Ice

Almost everyone owns a freezer, and in almost every freezer, you'll find ice. Ice can be a good source of drinkable water in emergencies. All you have to do is place the ice in a clean, leak-proof container and wait for it to melt.

2. Canned foods

Some canned foods are stored in a liquid that can be used to substitute as a safe water source. When you open up a can of fruit, vegetables, or even broth, don't waste the liquid. Drain it from the can, making sure to take out any solids, and store it for drinking.

3. Shelf stored beverages

Although not typically water, it can still be used as a drinkable liquid. Certain beverages like fruit juice, sports drinks, canned milk and milk boxes, and vegetable

juice have a long shelf life. You can store these in advance and use them as a substitute for water.

4. Toilet Flush Tank

This may seem unhygienic, but the water kept in the flush tank of your toilet is actually safe to drink as long as it hasn't been treated with any chemicals. Depending on the size of your toilet, there might be around 3 to 5 gallons of safe water store in the flush tank.

You can purify the water before drinking or using it, and never use the water from inside the toilet bowl.

5. Hot water heaters

Water heaters and hot water tanks are an excellent source of drinkable water in your house during an emergency. To avoid contamination of this water, make sure to turn off the main water valve in your house as soon as an event occurs.

Depending on the size of your water heater or hot water tank, it could be storing between 20 and 50 gallons of safe drinking water. Be careful when opening it to drain the water and make sure to use any instructions you have available.

Water Sources Outside Your Home

1. Rainwater

Rain is usually clean and safe to drink as it falls from the sky, as long as there have been no events that have contaminated the air or raised the pollution in your area. Catching rain and safely storing it can be an excellent source of water in an emergency.

2. Plants

It might be hard to believe, but there are methods of extracting water from plants. This method is called transpiration. You place a plastic bag over a tree branch or bush sitting somewhere in the sun. This causes condensation. In an hour or so, the water will start to condense on the sides of the plastic bag. This is a slow

process, and after about 5 hours, you'll be able to collect up to ½ cup of water.

Careful which plants you choose to extract water from, as some can contain toxins.

3. Solar still

This takes the same practice used on plants, but utilizes it in a different way. Start by digging a bowl-shaped hols directly beneath the sun. Create a dent at the bottom of the hole in the middle. This is where you'll place the container that you plan on using to capture the water. Now, fill the hole with non-toxic green plants. Cover the top of the hole with a clear, plastic sheet and use a small rock to weigh down the sides and the middle to create a small dent.

The still shape of the structure will force the condensation collecting on the plastic sheeting to slide towards the middle of the sheeting and drip into the container you have at the bottom of the hole.

4. Natural bodies of water

In an extreme emergency case, a natural body of water found in your surrounding area might be your best option for clean, drinkable water. Streams and rivers that are flowing downhill are safe to collect from, as long as you consider what is uphill of them. Waste of all kinds will often find their way into the water system.

Stagnant water that is found in ponds and lakes is not safe to drink as it is most likely contaminated. Avoid flood waters and water from swampy areas or marshes.

Water Purification

When you can't find any clean, drinkable water sources, then making your own clean water is the only other way to go. There are many ways you can purify and treat unclean water. The water you get from your tap is just used water that has been cleaned and purified. In dire situations, you can do the same.

BOOK 18

Boiling Water

A good, old fashioned way of purifying water and making it safe to drink is by boiling it. Boiling won't guarantee water that tastes good, but it will guarantee water free of contaminants.

Boiling the water won't take you very long at all, depending on the method you use. If you still have access to electricity, then using a kettle or stove is a good option. The kettle will be the fastes, but it will only boil a small amount of water. On the stove, you can boil a large amount of water, but it will take longer. If you don't have access to electricity, then fire is always a good method for boiling water. You can use a gas stove or build a campfire.

All these different methods mean different boiling point times for your water. However, a general rule to go by is once the water reaches the highest heat level, wait 10 minutes before removing it.

Make Your Own Filter

Water filtration systems are expensive, and they might be hard to come by in an emergency situation. If you don't already have one and you find yourself in need of one, you can always make your own.

All you need is:

1. **Sand**

2. **Charcoal**

3. **Rocks**

Take a clean sock or other straining container and add a layer of sand at the bottom, then add a layer of charcoal, and finally add a layer of rocks at the top. Place the sock over a container to catch the water and let the water slowly drain through the system that you've put together.

This method of filtration will reduce the amount of bacteria in the water and make it taste better. This method can not remove Giardia from the water.

Chlorination

Treating water with chlorine will kill most of the microorganisms inside the water. Of course, using this method means proper measurements because using too much chlorine can spell disaster.

There are three different methods you can use to purify your water through chlorination:

1. Potable Aqua tablets

These have been proven to be effective against viruses, bacteria, Lamblia, Giardia, Cryptosporidium, and other harmful microorganisms found in unsafe water. These are easy to use and can be added to your pantry for a rainy day. Just drop one tablet into your water and wait for it to take effect.

2. Chlorine bleach

You can use the same bleach you use to clean your house to clean your water. You need to measure out 1 spoonful of bleach to 1 gallon of water, more precisely, 10 drops of bleach to 1 gallon of water. Shake the water container and wait for the bleach to work. This will purify the water of almost anything, aside from Giardia.

When using bleach, be sure not to use scented bleach, bleach mixed with other cleaners, or color-safe bleach. Don't use pool chlorine, and always check the expiration date on the bottle first.

3. AquaMira water treatment drops

This is the same formula as in the Potable Aqua tablets, but with a much stronger mixture. 1 ounce of it can be used to treat and purify up to 30 gallons of water.

Remember, if you can't find clean drinking water, there is no need to panic. There are ways of cleaning your water and making it safe to drink. Even if you've found what seems to be clean drinking water, unless you are sure, it's always best to purify all your water using one of the above methods.

PREPPER'S PANTRY

  *Book 19*

Book 19:

Food

When it comes to the prepper lifestyle, there's usually one thing that they have an abundance of, and that's food. An experienced prepper has a pantry or storeroom stockpiled with food that has a long shelf life. That's the only way to properly prepare for an emergency. Food is an essential that we just can't go without. That's why, when a life altering event occurs, you'll want to be able to find food and properly store it so it lasts you a long time.

Let's face it, that store room stockpiled with food is going to run out eventually, and when that happens, there isn't going to be a quick run to the store for supplies. The only other option you have is to find your own food out in the wild.

Foraging for Food

Needing to forage through the forest and find food out in the wild means that you've entered desperate times. Desperate times call for desperate measures. It's not enough to be a skilled hunter or even a fisherman, although these skills can keep you well fed in times of need. You need to know the techniques and the tricks that many who are used to spending their time out in the wild use to stay fed and healthy.

Edible Flora

The first thing you can do is educate yourself on the edible and non-edible flora in your area. A lot of people focus too much on hunting down animals or catching fish in order to find food. There are simpler ways to stay fed. Fruits, berries, and nuts all grow in the wild, not just in your garden. If you can identify an edible fruit from a poisonous one, then you're in the money.

The easiest foods to get a hold of in the wild are nuts and fruits trees. When they grow, they grow in abundance. All you have to do is know how to identify them and how to find them in the wild. Then it's as easy as picking the low hanging fruit from its tree branch.

If nuts and fruits aren't available, there are always wild berries. Berries can't sustain a person's hunger but it can be enough to keep you going until you find other sources of food.

Berries are a bit more tricky since many of the edible berries resemble poisonous ones. As long as you know what to look out for, you can pick out the good from the bad.

Commons berries to avoid are:

- **Yew**

- **Holly**

- **Dogwood**

- **Pokeweed**

Common berries that you can eat are:

- **Gooseberries**

- **Muscadine**

- **Elderberries (if properly cooked)**

- **Mulberries**

If you're unsure whether something is edible or not, you can always perform an edible test. Most non-edible plants emit a strong, unpleasant odor. Divide something you want to test into different parts and smell each part. If the smell isn't strong or unpleasant, you can move on to the skin test. Rub a piece of the food up against a sensitive part of your skin, like your wrist. If there is no reaction, you can move on to the taste test. Eat a small piece of the food and wait to see if you have a reaction. Wait at least 15 minutes before you try to eat the food again.

This test should only be done as a last resort when you can't find any other food.

Creepy Crawlies

If you really can't find any other food to eat, then you may have to resort to eating those critters that crawl on the ground and hide in holes under rocks. These aren't the most appetizing of options, but if there's nothing else left to eat, you must do anything to survive.

Bugs are always going to be available ,and there's always going to be plenty of them. There are very few harmful and poisonous bugs, so you shouldn't have a problem picking some up to have as a meal. Bugs are also a great source of protein, which will keep you feeling fuller for longer.

Here are some general rules to follow when looking for edible bugs:

1. **If a bug has bright colors, avoid it.**

This is true for both bugs and other creatures as well. The most deadly creatures tend to be the most beautiful.

2. **Bugs that bite, sting, or have a lot of hair must be avoided.**

These kinds of bugs need to be eaten in a certain way or they can be harmful. If you don't have the correct knowledge, it's best to move on.

3. **If a bug smells really bad, avoid it.**

Some bugs, including the stink bug, are still edible despite their smell. However, most bugs that emit a strong, bad odor should be avoided.

How to Store Food

If you are able to find a reliable food source, whether it's through hunting, foraging, fishing, or gardening, you don't want any of that food going to waste. Storing your food properly can help you keep it fresh and edible for a longer amount of time, ensuring that no food is wasted.

There are multiple ways you can store your food to last longer. Each method works, but each method of storing food only works for a certain kind of food. For instance, salting meat can keep it preserved and help it last longer, but the same thing won't apply to fruit or vegetables.

Canning Food

Canning is a popular way of storing food for preppers for a few reasons:

1. **It's simple and easy.**

2. **It can be done in moments.**

3. **Canned food takes up little to no shelf space.**

4. **Almost everything from your garden can be stored in cans.**

If you haven't canned food before, don't worry, it's more simple than it sounds. All you need is access to preserve jars with tight, sealable lids, a Pressure Canner, and the food that you want to can. Almost all fruits and vegetables are the best for canning, and even some meats can be canned.

The pressure canning method is the safest for low-acid foods, such as meats and vegetables. Choosing the right method depends on the type of food you plan on storing in cans.

PRESSURE CANNER

There are two methods for packing the food into cans. These are:

1. **Raw pack method.**

In this method, raw and unheated food is put directly in the jar and boiling water, syrup, or juice is poured over the food. When this is done, fruit and vegetables will shrink, so they should be packed tightly. Corn, potatoes, peas, and lima beans should be packed loosely because they expand.

2. **Hot pack method.**

For this method, food is heated to boiling point or cooked for a specific time before being packed into the jar with the hot liquid. In this method, the shrinking has already taken place, so all food can be packed loosely to allow the liquid to surround it.

Pressure Canning Method

There should be instructions that come with your pressure canner; be sure to read them before you start canning any food.

First, pour 2 to 3 inches of water into your canner. The water needs to be hot, but it shouldn't be boiling if you're canning raw packed food. If you're canning hot packed food, then the water should be hot or gently boiling.

Next, fill your jars with food as described in the different packing methods. No matter which method you choose, you need to allow for space at the top of the jar, so don't fill to the brim, remove all the air bubbles by lightly tapping the outside of the jar, wipe the rims, and place the lid on the jar.

Place the jars on the rack inside your canner, allowing for space between each jar for the steam to flow. Close the canner tightly so no steam can escape from anywhere other than the vent. Turn the heat on the canner to high and wait for steam to start escaping from the vent. Let this go on for at least 10 minutes to allow for excess air from the jars to escape.

After 10 minutes have passed, close the vent. Depending on the type of canner you have, you'll have a dial-gauge or a weighted-gauge. For a weighted-gauge, just make sure you're using the right pressure. For a dial-gauge, allow the pressure to rise to 8 pounds of pressure then lower the temperature slightly until the pressure rises to the correct pressure.

As soon as you have the correct pressure, you can start counting the processing time. The processing time depends on the food you're canning and what recipe you're using. Watch the canner and change the temperature regularly, lowering or raising it depending on the pressure change. You want to keep the pressure at the correct point according to your recipe.

Do not open the canner at any time or this will lead to a loss of pressure and the whole process needs to start over again.

When the processing time is done, turn off your canner and wait 30 minutes to an hour for the pressure in the canner to drop to zero. When this happens, you can take off the lid and start removing your newly canned food.

BOOK 19

Freezing Food

In a bugging out situation, freezing food is probably the last thing you'll think of. However, the experienced prepper will always plan to bug in unless circumstances make it impossible to do so. If you're bugging in, then freezing your food is the best choice in preserving its freshness and extending its shelf life.

There are some disadvantages to using a freezer for preserving your food supply:

- **Loss of power renders your freezer useless.**

- **Frozen food loses its quality.**

- **Chance of freezer burn.**

- **Forgetting what food you have.**

Along with these disadvantages, there are plenty of advantages to think of as well:

- **Freezing extends shelf-life indefinitely.**

- **Reduces food waste.**

- **Saves time when you're preserving and storing large amounts of food.**

- **Preserves the nutrient content.**

- **Easily store homemade and ready-to-eat meals.**

- **Prevents microbes from spreading.**

As you can see, the many advantages outweigh the few disadvantages. Meaning that freezing your survival food is a good choice. That being said, you can't store every food item you have in your freezer. Some food doesn't freeze well and defrosts even worse. The type of foods that will live a long and healthy life in your freezer are:

1. Meat, poultry, and fish

2. Certain fresh and processed vegetables and fruits

3. Dairy Products

4. Pantry Staples (rice, flour, nuts, seeds, etc.)

5. Eggs (powdered, boiled, or cooked)

6. Bread (including cakes and pies)

7. Juice

8. Ready-to-eat meals (soups, pasta, boxed pizzas, etc.)

9. Beans

10. Leftovers

There are very few foods that don't do well in freezers. However, there are a few foods that should never be frozen due to the thawing process that could end up in a mess of inedible food.

1. Never freeze eggs still in their shell.

2. Cream based products will separate when thawed (mayonnaise).

3. Starch thickened stews or gravy will also separate when thawed.

4. Water vegetables and fruits should not be frozen (cucumber, celery, lettuce, etc.).

5. Canned goods that are still in a sealed can should not be frozen.

6. Carbonated drinks should never be frozen.

7. Pre-fried food will become soggy when thawed.

BOOK 19

Dehydrating Food

Dehydrating your food is the easiest way to preserve it. This method has been used for thousands of years to help keep food fresh and edible without the need of a fridge or freezer. Dehydrating is the fastest and most inexpensive way to make your food last. It also makes food lighter for traveling and takes up less space for storing.

Dehydrating Methods

There are multiple ways to dehydrate your food. Some ways are far more simple, some take a lot longer, and others are fast and efficient but require certain tools and equipment you might not have access to.

1. Sun drying

In this method. fruit is sliced thinly and placed on a rack in the sun. This works in places that have long periods of time with hot, uninterrupted sunshine. Anywhere with a humidity level of 60% and a minimum temperature of 86 degrees Fahrenheit will also work.

2. Air drying

Air drying is similar to sun drying, where the food is hung out in the open to dry, but with air drying, the food is usually hung in the shade. This is used for foods such as herbs and delicate green vegetables that need protection from the sun.

3. Oven drying

This method uses an oven set to 140 degrees Fahrenheit to slowly dry out food. Meat must be cut thinly and cooked ahead of time before being placed on a tray in the oven. The door needs to be kept open and the oven has to stay around 140 degrees Fahrenheit. Any higher and your food will cook instead of dry.

Best Food for Dehydrating

Not all foods work well for dehydrating, but most foods can survive the process and still end up tasting great.

- **Vegetables like mushrooms, carrots, peas, onions, tomatoes, and beans**

- **Fruit like apricots, apples, cherries, bananas, blueberries and pears**

- **Nuts and seeds**

- **Herbs**

- **Sprouted grains like rice, amaranth, and barley**

- **Meat and fish**

- **Bread and crackers**

THE
PREPPER'S
COOKBOOK

Introduction

Imagine a world where you're forced to live off of the food from your garden or on the food stockpiled in cans and frozen in freezers. A world like that seems tasteless. It seems bland and boring when all you have to look forward to is a can of soup, heated up and thrown into a bowl. It doesn't have to be that way.

If there is one thing preppers know, it's how to get creative with food. Cooking for you and your family from your emergency pantry doesn't have to be as simple as opening up a can or cutting up the vegetables from your garden.

In an emergency situation, you're already dealing with so much; tasteless and bland food doesn't have to be one of those things.

THE PREPPER'S COOKBOK

  **Book 20**

Book 20:

Recipes for Breakfast

Breakfast is the most important meal of the day. It gives us the energy we need to get the day started and sets the mood for the entire day ahead of us. A bad breakfast usually means there's a bad day ahead. That's why making sure you have a tasty and satisfying breakfast is important.

Most of these recipes go with the fact that you have access to the foods and staples mentioned. Some of the ingredients in the recipes can be found in your prepper's pantry while others can be sourced from your homestead animals or your garden if you have them. All fresh ingredients can be substituted for canned or long-life options.

Pancakes

Pancakes are a simple and delicious start to the day. Most ingredients can be found fresh or even on your pantry shelves. Pancakes can also be cooked on a stove, if you have one available, or over a fire.

They take only a few minutes of prep and cook time and there are multiple toppings that can be added for flavor. You'll need few ingredients. Discover the whole recipe on the next page.

Pancakes

COOK: 10 MIN

PREP: 5 MIN

SERVINGS: 4

Ingredients:

- **1 cup all-purpose Flour** (a common staple for preppers)

- **1 Egg, beaten** (fresh from your livestock or powdered)

- **2 tablespoons white Sugar** (a common staple for peppers)

- **1 cup Milk** (fresh from your livestock or powdered, can also be substituted with water)

- **2 teaspoons Baking powder** (a commons staple for preppers)

- **2 tablespoons vegetable Oil** (canned butter can be used as a substitute)

- **1 teaspoon salt**

Cooking instructions

Mix all the ingredients together one by one, adding the dry ingredients first and then the wet ingredients. If using powdered eggs and powdered milk, then some water will be needed to activate the ingredients. The mixture needs to be thick but runny. Mix until there are no lumps and all ingredients have blended fully.

Grease the cooking surface with the oil or canned butter. Pour or scoop the batter on the griddle, using approximately 1/4 cup for each pancake. Wait until you see bubbles forming on top of the mixture before flipping the pancake over. Brown on both sides and serve hot.

When your pancakes are done, there are a number of toppings you can use:

- **Maple syrup** (this has an almost indefinite shelf life and should be a part of your pantry)
- **Chocolate chips** (if stored correctly, these last a long time)
- **Fruit** (these can be freeze-dried, canned, or fresh from your garden)
- **Sugar and cinnamon** (these staples have a long shelf life)
- **Honey** (similar to maple syrup with an indefinite shelf life)

All of the ingredients in this recipe can be substituted with a pancake mix, which has a long shelf life and can be added to your pantry.

Oatmeal

Oatmeal is a great staple with a long shelf life and a great source of protein and fiber. The perfect start to any day. Quick rolled oats will last the longest in your pantry, and they can be used for multiple recipes, not just breakfast.

Oatmeal is a great way to start the day and only takes a few minutes to make.

Oatmeal

COOK: 5 MIN

PREP: 5 MIN

SERVINGS: 4

Ingredients:

- **4 cup of Rolled oats** (this should be in your pantry)

- **2 cup milk**(fresh from your livestock or powdered)

- **2 cup Water** as much as necessary (bottled or boiled water works well)

- **1/8 teaspoon kosher Salt** (a long shelf life ingredient that should be in your pantry)

- **1/2 teaspoon ground cinnamon**

- **Desired toppings** (such as sliced almonds, peanut butter, or fresh fruit)

Cooking instructions:

1.   Measure out enough oatmeal for each person that will be eating it. One cup per person is a good measurement. Place the oats in a pot large enough to cook and place over the fire or stove. Add, milk, water, salt and cinnamon.

2.   Bring to a boil, then reduce heat to low. The oats should be soft and the water should be completely gone when the oats are cooked. If the water is gone but the oats still seem dry, you can add some more water and repeat the process. Once the oats are done, you can add several toppings for taste:

- **Fruit** (freeze-dried, canned, or fresh from your garden)
- **Maple syrup**
- **Milk** (fresh from your livestock or powdered)
- **Sugar**
- **Butter**
- **Honey**

Eggs and Toast

Eggs and toast is a good, old fashioned breakfast that has been waking people up in the morning and getting them ready for the day for centuries. Bread lasts long if frozen correctly, but you can even make your own bread with staples you can find in your pantry.

Eggs can be collected fresh from your livestock, or powdered eggs from your pantry can be used. You can use peanut butter on your toast, which is a great staple, or you can use canned butter.

Consider adding a cup of tea, coffee, or fruit juice to this breakfast. All options can be found in your pantry since they have long shelf lives.

Sunny side up Eggs

COOK: 5 MIN

PREP: 3 MIN

SERVINGS: 4

Ingredients:

- 1 egg for each person

- 1/2 tablespoon of butter

- A pinch of kosher Salt and a sprinkle of black Pepper.

Cooking instructions:

You'll want to cook eggs on medium low or low heat. The slower the better with eggs, since they're delicate and can easily be overcooked. Here are the basic steps to a perfectly cooked sunny side up egg. Heat ½ tablespoon butter over medium low heat. Add 1 or 2 eggs and sprinkle with a pinch of kosher salt and a few grinds black peopper. Cook for 2 to 3 minutes, until the whites are firm but the yolk is still runny. Don't flip them.

     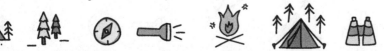

COOK: 40 MIN

PREP: 8 MIN

SERVINGS: 4

Making Bread

Making bread and freezing it for your morning toast can save you time and energy in the morning. You'll need few ingredients:

Ingredients:

- **2 cups warm Water** (bottled or boiled water works well)

- **5 or 6 cups Flour** (a common staple for peppers)

- **1/2 cup Sugar** (a common staple for peppers)

- **1/4 cup Oil**

- **1 ½ tablespoons yeast**

- **1 ½ teaspoons salt**

Cooking instructions:

Dissolve the sugar into a large bowl with the warm water and then stir in the yeast. Let it sit for five minutes so the yeast can proof. Mix in the salt and oil and then mix in the flour one cup at a time. Mix until the mixture resembles a dough.

Knead the dough for around 7 minutes and then place in an oiled bowl. Cover the bowl with a damp cloth and allow it to sit for an hour so the dough can rise. It should double in size.

Knead the dough for about 1 minute before cutting it in half. Shape each half into a loaf and then place them each in a loaf pan and allow to sit for 30 minutes. Then place in an oven set to 350 degrees Fahrenheit for 30 to 40 minutes.

Allow to cool before cutting into your bread and eating it.

THE PREPPER'S COOKBOOK

  *Book 21*

Book 21:

Recipes for Lunch

Lunches should be light and filled with protein for energy. A successful lunch can be made and eaten in less than an hour. It shouldn't be too filling or else dinner later that day will be ruined, but it shouldn't be too light or it's just a snack. The best lunches are ones that don't need to be cooked and can be eaten on the go.

Sandwiches

Sandwiches are a simple and tasty food to keep your energy up without being too filling and heavy. This is a great meal, especially if you've taken the time to make your own bread. Here are some things, you can put on bread for sandwiches:

- **Tuna** (canned tuna is an excellent staple to add to your pantry)

- **Chicken mayo** (chicken can be frozen, making it last longer, and mayo is an excellent staple)

- **Tomato and cheese** (tomatoes can be fresh from your garden or canned, and cheese can be powdered or processed slices)

- **Peanut butter and syrup** (peanut butter and maple syrup both have a long shelf life)

Whether the ingredients are fresh, canned, or frozen, a good sandwich can keep you going until that big, hot meal that is waiting for you at the end of the day.

Sandwiches

COOK: 10 MIN

PREP: 5 MIN

SERVINGS: 4

Ingredients:

- **2 (5 oz.)** Cans Chunk Light or Albacore White **Tuna** (chunked and drained)

- 1/4 cup mayonnaise

- 1 hard cooked egg, chopped

- 2 tsp. lemon juice

- 1/2 cup chopped celery

- Lettuce leaves, curly-leaf

- 8 slices bread

Cooking instructions:

In a medium bowl, combine all ingredients except bread and lettuce; mix well. Chill several hours. Line 4 slices bread with lettuce; top each with 1/4 tuna mixture and top with remaining bread.

COOK: 15 MIN

PREP: 15 MIN

SERVINGS: 4

Cream of Soup

Soup is just as quick and easy to make as it is to eat. Soups pack a punch of energy as well as tasting excellent. They can be sweet, savory, healthy, or all of the above. Soups can be made from fresh ingredients or dried, canned, and packed staple ingredients.

You'll need these ingredients:

Ingredients:

- **2 cups of Milk** (fresh or powdered)

- **6 tablespoons all-purpose flour**

- **½ cup butter**

- **2 cubes chicken bouillon**

- **Herbs**

- **Salt and pepper**

Cooking instructions:

Melt butter in a saucepan. Add flour and make a paste. Add milk and bouillon cubes. Cook over low heat until thickened. Add pepper to taste. Add more milk when adding the other soup ingredients, depending on the thickness you desire.

At this point, you can add whatever you want to the soup. Some good options are:

- **Mushrooms** (canned or fresh)

- **Tomatoes** (canned or fresh)

- **Onions** (canned or fresh)

- **Peas** (canned or fresh)

- **Carrots** (canned or fresh)

You can spice up the soup a little more by adding croutons, which is an easy addition if you've learned how to make your own bread.

THE PREPPER'S COOKBOOK

  *Book 22*

Book 22:

Recipes for Dinner

A good dinner needs to have certain qualities. It needs to be comfortable food that makes you breathe a sigh of relief as you sit down and prepare for the rest of the night. It needs to be filling, because you've spent all the energy you throughout the day and now you want a full belly to help you rest. It needs to be hot and tasty, because you deserve a hot and delicious meal after a long, hard day.

The dinner you make out of your survival pantry can be all of these things, as long as you're creative enough.

Pizza

Pizza is a dish of Italian origin consisting of a usually round, flat base of leavened wheat-based dough topped with tomatoes, cheese, and often various other ingredients (such as anchovies, mushrooms, onlns, olives, vegetables, meat, ham, etc.), which is then baked at a high temperature, traditionally in a wood-fired oven.

Everybody loves pizza, and you can make your own pizza at home with the ingredients you have in your survival pantry.

Pizza

COOK: 20 MIN

PREP: 30 MIN

SERVINGS: 4

Ingredients:

For the crust, you'll need:

- 2 cups of flour

- 1 cup water

- 1 teaspoon baking powder

- 1 teaspoon sugar

- ¼ teaspoon salt

- Oil

For the sauce, you'll need:

- **Tomatoes** (fresh from the garden or canned)

For the toppings, you'll need:

- **Oil**

- **Mushrooms** (fresh or canned)

- **Meat of your choosing** (frozen or canned)

- **Cheese** (parmesan lasts long, but you can also use powdered cheese)

Cooking instructions:

For the crust, you need to mix all the dry ingredients together and blend them with a fork. Use the fork to make a well in the middle and pour in some oil and the water. Mix it all together until it forms a dough. Knead the dough into a ball and let it rest for 20 minutes beneath a damp cloth.

Once the dough is ready, form it into a pizza shape and pour the tomato mixture over the top for the sauce. Now, add your toppings as generously as you want and throw the pizza into the oven.Pizza cooks quickly as long as the base is thin enough. Bake pizza in the 392°F oven, until the crust is browned and the cheese is golden, about 20 minutes.

COOK: 10 MIN

PREP: 20 MIN

SERVINGS: 4

Beef or Chicken Stew

Beef or Chicken Stew

There's nothing better than a hot, hearty stew after a long day's work. Stew is easy to come by in a survival situation, as long as you have taken care to add

canned beef or chicken stew to your survival pantry. You'll need:

Ingredients:

- 2 Canned beef or chicken stew

- Fresh or canned vegetables

- Canned tomatoes or freshly diced ones

- Herbs for seasoning

Cooking instructions:

Empty your can of stew into a pot and add the vegetables and tomatoes. Stir well on a medium heat for around 10 minutes, or until the mixture begins to boil. You can add croutons, onions, or even potatoes if you have them in your garden to add flavor to the stew.

COOK: 2 HOURS

PREP: 20 MIN

SERVINGS: 4

Chicken Broth and Dumplings

Dumplings area thick and filling treat to add to your evening meal. Chicken broth is simple to make and can be a nice, hot meal filled with nutrients to help you rest.

This easy recipe for Chicken and Dumplings is the ideal comfort food. A hearty recipe that uses chicken, and dumplings that's both simple to make and shockingly easy to lose yourself in for a moment or two.

Ingredients:

For the broth, you'll need:

- **Chicken** (dried, frozen, or canned)

- **Vegetables** (fresh, dried, or canned)

- **Herbs and spices**

- **Cornstarch**

- **Chicken stock**

- **Water**

For the dumplings, you'll need:

- **1 cup flour**

- **2 tablespoons butter** (canned)

- **Salt**

- **Water or powdered milk**

Cooking instructions:

1. For the broth, combine all the ingredients together in a pot and stir on a low heat until everything is tender and the flavor from the ingredients has seeped into the water.

2. For the dumplings, mix the ingredients together until you've created a soft dough and then add the dumplings one by one to the cooked and still hot broth. Allow them to simmer until they are cooked.

3. Your meal is ready to be served and enjoyed.

COOK: 5 MIN

PREP: 10 MIN

SERVINGS: 4

Mac and Cheese

This is a dish that has been loved by children and adults alike. It's a simple dish that requires only 3 ingredients to make and can be garnished by anything you have available.

Ingredients:

- Dry pasta

- Sachet of cheese sauce

- Water

Cooking instructions:

Fill a pot with water and let it boil before adding the pasta. The pasta should be soft and cooked in 5 minutes or less. Drain the water and add the cheese sauce to the pasta. Mix together on a low heat, and your meal is done.

To garnish this meal, you can add the following toppings:

- **Herbs for flavor**

- **Canned or frozen pieces of meat**

- **Powdered cheese for extra cheesy flavor**

- **Canned or fresh tomatoes**

THE PREPPER'S COOKBOOK

  *Book 23*

Book 23:

Snacks and Desserts

It's not an easy task, learning how to survive. You have to get used to doing things yourself, rationing your food, living below your means, and taking one day at a time. When something like this happens and we're forced to change the way we live our lives, it might be hard for some people to adjust.

One thing we can do to make it a little easier is hold on to the small things that used to bring us joy and happiness. For most, that small thing was a tasty snack or a delicious dessert.

Peanut Butter Oat Cookies

Ingredients:

- 1 1/2 cups old fashioned oats

- 1/2 cup all-purpose flour

- 1/2 teaspoon baking soda

- 1/4 teaspoon salt

- 1/2 teaspoon ground cinnamon

- 1/2 cup unsalted butter at room temperature

- 1/2 cup creamy peanut butter

- 1/2 cup granulated sugar

- 1/2 cup light brown sugar

- 1 large egg

- 1 teaspoon vanilla extract

Peanut Butter Oat Cookies

COOK: 12 MIN

PREP: 15 MIN

COOKIES: 18

Cooking instructions:

Prehewat the oven to 350 degrees F. Line two large baking sheet with Silpat baking mats or parchment paper. Set aside. In a medium bowl, whisk together the oats, flour, baking soda, salt, and cinnamon. Set aside.

Using a mixer, beat the butter, peanut butter, and sugars together until creamy, this will take about 2 minutes, on medium speed. Beat in the egg and vanilla extract. Mix until well combined. On low, add in the dry ingredients and mix until just until the combined.

Scoop the cookies into round balls and place on the prepared baking sheets, leaving 2 inches in between cookies. Bake for 10-12 minutes, or until the cookies are lightly browned around the edges, but still soft in the middle.

Remove cookies from oven and let cool on the baking sheet for about 5 minutes. Transfer to a wire rack and cool completely.

Honey Nut Snacks

Nuts and honey or maple syrup should be a crucial part of your prepper's pantry. Nuts are stuffed with protein and tend to last very long if packed correctly. Maple syrup and honey have an indefinite shelf life, so it's more than likely you'll have these things available.

All you need is nuts and honey or maple syrup, and cinnamon is an optional addition.

Empty your nuts (it can be peanuts, walnuts, or cashew nuts) into a bowl. Pour in some honey or maple syrup and toss the nuts around with your hands. You want the nuts to be completely coated with the honey or maple syrup.

When they are coated, you can spread the nuts out on a greased tray. Make sure none of them are on top of one another. You can sprinkle a little bit of cinnamon over the top of the nuts for a spicy flavor.

Place the tray in the oven on a very low heat and leave the door open. Alternatively, you can place the tray over a fire, high enough so that the flames do not touch the bottom of the tray. You want the nuts to roast and the honey coating to dry. Too hot or too close to the fire and both will burn.

Veggie Crisps

Not everyone is a fan of vegetables, but everyone loves crisps. You can combine the two in an easy to make veggie crisp snack. This can be done with plenty of vegetables. The best vegetables to do this with are:

- **Carrots**

- **Kale**

- **Buttersquash**

- **Cucumber**

If you are growing these vegetables in your garden, then all you have to do is cut them into thin slices and spread those slices onto a greased tray. Sprinkle some sugar over the top and slide it into an oven on a low heat or high over a fire. You. want to wait for the moisture to be drawn from the vegetables and for them to become crispy.

This works for some fruits as well like bananas and apples.

MEAL PLAN AND
SHOPPING LIST

MEAL PLAN AND SHOPPING LIST

Prepper's
Shopping
List

  **Book 25**

Book 24:

A Prepper's Shopping List

Getting prepared for an emergency may seem overwhelming at first. You have to make a plan, source out the food you need, stockpile the food, and make sure you have enough to last you and your family. That's a lot to take it all at once. However, the easiest thing you can do is make a list. Once you have a list, it all gets easier from there.

There are indeed a lot of factors to consider when building an emergency food supply for you and your family. The hardest part is knowing what foods to stockpile and what foods to avoid.

Canned Food

Canned food is easily the most well known prepper food. Its shelf life is usually years from purchase as long as it's not opened. Canned food is also a prepper favorite due to how little space they take up and how easily stackable they are.

The only downside of canned food is they tend to be very unhealthy. They have a very high sodium content, and even the canned fruits have a lot of syrups and sugars. Canned food also tends to be bland and mushy, especially when it comes to the canned vegetables. However, preppers plan for disasters, and when you're in the middle of a disaster, you can't complain about what you have or don't have to eat.

Canned food options include:

- **Canned fish (tuna, sardines, etc.)**

- Canned soups

- Canned ready-to-eat meals (tinned spaghetti, etc.)

- Canned meats (Spam, chicken, meatballs, etc.)

- Canned spray cheese

- Canned fruits

- Canned Vegetables

- Canned beans and lentils

- Canned dairy (coconut milk or condensed milk)

Jars

A general rule is that anything packed into a jar has a long shelf life. This is because most jar packed foods are expected to stay in the stores for a while, so preservatives are added to them to make them last longer.

The downside to jars is their packaging. Generally, preppers tend to stay away from anything that is packed in a container that can break. Since jars are made of glass, there is always a risk of shattering. If you can find some of these foods in plastic containers, it would be better.

Jarred options include:

- Peanut butter and nutella (other nut based butters as well)

- Jam and jelly

- Sauces (ketchup, soy sauce, mayo, BBQ sauce, salad dressing, etc.)

- Tomato or pasta sauces

   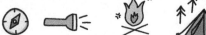

BOOK 24

Starches and Grains

You get most of your energy from carbohydrates, and they help you feel full for longer. They can also help other foods taste a lot better.

The downside to these foods is the way they are stored. When you buy grains or starchy foods, they're usually stored in cardboard boxes or plastic bags. These are okay for short term, but for long term storage, you'll see your food ravaged by moths and bugs or destroyed by moisture.

Repackage the food as you buy it into tightly sealed, water-proof plastic containers.

Food options are:

- Flour
- Baking powder
- Yeast
- Baking soda
- Rice
- Pasta
- Crackers
- Oats
- Cereals
- Whole grains
- Couscous
- Instant mashed potatoes
- Cocoa powder

Protein

Protein is an extremely important part of any diet. It gives us energy, helps us feel full, and many other benefits. The most mentioned prepper food for protein is beans, but these aren't as great as people are led to believe. The main reason being that it takes hours to properly cook beans.

Options for protein include:

- Dry lentils (these are much faster to cook than beans)

- Jerky

- Nuts and seeds

- Powdered eggs

- Canned cheese or waxed wheel cheese

- Canned peas or chickpeas

- Protein bars

Crucial Stocks

Other crucial stocks that should be kept in your household include:

- **Coffee and tea**

- **Sugar**

- **Honey**

- **Salt and pepper**

- **Oil**

- **Herbs and spices**

- **Powdered milk**

- **Instant drink mixes**

- **Sports drinks**

- **Fruit juice**

MEAL PLAN AND SHOPPING LIST

monday

tuesday

Book 25:

A Prepper's Meal Plan

Week 1

	BREAKFAST	LUNCH	SNACK	DINNER
MONDAY	Oatmeal	Chicken & Mayo Sandwich	Veggie Crisps	Beans & Rice
TUESDAY	Blueberry Pancakes	Soup & Croutons	Trail Mix	Mac & Cheese
WEDNESDAY	Fruit Salad	Mac & Cheese Leftovers	Protein Bar	Chicken & Dumplings
THURSDAY	Eggs&Toast	Tomato & Cheese Toasted Sandwich	PB on Toast	Beef Stew
FRIDAY	Protein/ Fruit Smoothie	Leftover Beef Stew & Pasta	PB & Oat Cookies	Lemon Grilled Fish & Veg
SATURDAY	Cereal & coconut milk	Grilled Chicken & Bread	Coffee or Tea	Meat Kebabs & Roasted Veg
SUNDAY	Coffee or Tea & Muffins	Tuna Sandwich	Honey Nuts	Pizza

Week 2

	BREAKFAST	LUNCH	SNACK	DINNER
MONDAY	Eggs on Toast	Leftover Pizza	Trail Mix	Beans & Rice
TUESDAY	Oatmeal with fruit	Tuna Sandwich	Fresh Fruit or Nuts	Pizza
WEDNESDAY	Coffee or Tea & Muffins	Cream of Soup	Protein Bar	Beef Stew & Dumplings
THURSDAY	Fruit Salad	Leftover Stew with Pasta	Crackers and Cheese	Beans & Rice
FRIDAY	Cinnamon Pancakes	Leftover Beans & Rice	Veggie Crisps	Grilled Fish & Spiced Rice
SATURDAY	Porridge with Coconut Milk	Toasted Cheese Sandwich	Honey Nuts	Chicken Broth, Rice, & Veg
SUNDAY	Protein/ Fruit Smoothie	Grilled Chicken & Bread	Jelly with Fruit Pieces	Mac & Cheese

Week 3

	BREAKFAST	LUNCH	SNACK	DINNER
MONDAY	Cereal with Coconut Milk	Leftover Mac&Cheese	Buttered Crackers	Fish and Roasted Veg
TUESDAY	Blueberry Pancakes	Chicken & Mayo Toasted Sandwich	Tea or Coffee	Meat Kebabs & Spiced Rice
WEDNESDAY	Fruit Salad	Soup with Croutons	PB & Oat Cookies	Pizza
THURSDAY	Oatmeal	Leftover Pizza	Veggie Crisps	Roast Chicken, Rice, & Veg
FRIDAY	Coffee or Tea & Muffins	Tuna Sandwich	Honey Nuts	Pasta with Canned Tomatoes
SATURDAY	Protein/ Fruit Smoothie	Leftover Pasta	Jelly	Chicken Broth & Dumplings
SUNDAY	Egg on Toast	Leftover Chicken Broth with Rice	Protein Bar	Beef Stew

Week 4

	BREAKFAST	LUNCH	SNACK	DINNER
MONDAY	Oatmeal with fruit	Soup with Toast	Honey Nuts	Mac and Cheese
TUESDAY	Coffee or Tea with Toast	Cheese Toasted Sandwich	Jelly with Fruit	Grilled Fish and Veg
WEDNESDAY	Protein/ Fruit Smoothie	Tuna Sandwich	Veggie Crisps	Chicken Stew & Dumplings
THURSDAY	Cinnamon Pancakes	Leftover Chicken Stew with Rice	PB or Jam on Toast	Meat Kebabs & Spiced Rice
FRIDAY	Egg on Toast	Chicken & Mayo Toasted Sandwich	Protein Bar	Beef Stew
SATURDAY	Cereal with Coconut Milk	Coffee or Tea & Toast	Crackers and Cheese	Beans&Rice
SUNDAY	Coffee or Tea & Muffins	Leftover Beans&Rice	PB & Oat Cookies	Pizza

RENEWABLE ENERGY SOLUTIONS

  *Book 26*

Book 26:

Renewable Energy Solutions

As the world recognizes the need for a sustainable and environmentally friendly energy landscape, renewable energy sources have become more important than ever. Some of the more significant sustainable energy methods being developed for future use include solar energy, wind energy, hydroelectric power, geothermal energy, bioenergy, ocean energy, hydrogen, and fuel cells. Solar energy, wind energy and hydroelectric energy devices are recommended to be in your possession prior to a preppers scenario.

How to Use Solar Energy

Solar energy is the cleanest and most abundant energy source today. It works by using sunlight to produce electrical energy. Its recommended that you purchase a solar-powered station for your prepping needs in advance of an off-grid scenario and its essential to understand the different wattages and the devices they can power. A 100-watt solar panel can generate around 400 watt-hours of energy per day, assuming 4 hours of direct sunlight. This is sufficient to charge small devices like smartphones, tablets, or LED lights for several hours. A 200-watt solar panel setup can produce approximately 800 watt-hours daily, which can power a small refrigerator for a few hours, run a laptop for a full day, or charge larger batteries.

For more demanding applications, consider a 500-watt solar array. This can generate around 2,000 watt-hours per day, enough to power a small TV, a few lights, and a laptop simultaneously. It can also run power tools intermittently. A 1,000-watt solar station is ideal for powering larger appliances like a full-sized refrigerator, a washing machine, or a well pump for several hours a day.

When designing your solar-powered station, consider your energy needs and the devices you'll be running. Invest in high-quality, deep-cycle batteries to store the generated energy for later use. Remember to include a charge controller and an inverter to regulate the power flow and convert the DC power from the batteries to AC power for your appliances. With proper planning and the right components, a solar-powered station can provide reliable, sustainable energy for your prepping needs.

How to Use Wind Energy

Wind energy uses wind turbines to collect and convert kinetic energy from the wind that we encounter when we are outside into electrical energy for maintaining power grids. It is mainly used on farms or homes in rural areas. There are two types of farms that apply wind energy to keep things running.

When considering a wind turbine generator for your prepping needs, it's crucial to understand the various wattages and the devices they can power. A small 400-watt wind turbine can generate around 1.2 kilowatt-hours (kWh) of energy per day in an area with average wind speeds of 12 mph. This is enough to charge a smartphone for a month, run a few LED lights for several hours, or power a small laptop for a full day.

A 1,000-watt wind turbine can produce approximately 3 kWh of energy daily under the same wind conditions. This can power a small refrigerator for a day, run a TV for several hours, or charge power tool batteries. For larger energy demands, a 2,000-watt wind turbine can generate around 6 kWh per day, sufficient to power a washing machine for a couple of hours, run a small water pump, or maintain a small home office setup.

When setting up your wind turbine generator, consider your location's average wind speeds and the height at which you'll install the turbine. Higher altitudes generally provide more consistent wind speeds. Invest in quality batteries to store the generated energy and ensure you have a charge controller to regulate the power flow. With proper installation and maintenance, a wind turbine generator can provide a reliable, renewable energy source for your prepping needs, especially when combined with other power sources like solar panels.

How to Use Hydroelectric Power

As one of the oldest forms of renewable energy, hydroelectric power uses the strength of water to generate electricity. Dams, reservoirs, and run-of-river systems are the most common uses for hydroelectric power. For dams, water is released from the dam to spin turbines and generate electricity. Reservoirs hold potential energy that produces electricity behind the dams. River systems generate electricity by diverting a portion of a river's flow through turbines,

In a prepping scenario, a water flow turbine generator can provide a reliable source of renewable energy, especially if you have access to a steady stream or river. The wattage output of these generators varies depending on the water flow rate and the turbine's size. A small, portable 500-watt water turbine can generate around 2 kilowatt-hours (kWh) of energy per day, assuming a flow rate of 5 gallons per minute. This is sufficient to charge a smartphone for several weeks, power a small fridge for a day, or run a few LED lights for extended periods.

A larger, 1,500-watt water turbine can produce approximately 6 kWh of energy per day under the same flow conditions. This can power a small water filtration system for several hours, run a laptop and a TV simultaneously, or charge larger battery banks for later use. For more substantial energy needs, a 5,000-watt

water turbine can generate around 20 kWh per day, enough to power a small off-grid cabin, run power tools, or maintain a small greenhouse.

When incorporating a water flow turbine generator into your prepping plans, consider the accessibility and reliability of the water source. Ensure proper installation and secure anchoring to prevent damage during high-flow events. Invest in quality batteries and a charge controller to store and regulate the generated power. With careful planning and maintenance, a water flow turbine generator can provide a dependable, renewable energy source for your prepping needs.

NAVIGATION TECHNIQUES

  *Book 27*

Book 27:

Navigation Techniques

You're driving out in the middle of nowhere on a dangerous terrain, say, the mountains. The weather is heavy with snow and ice. What do you do to keep from getting lost or in danger? Realize that navigating the outdoors requires a combination of tools and techniques to ensure you stay on course and reach your destination safely. Here are some essential navigation techniques:

Map Reading

You're driving out in the middle of nowhere on a dangerous terrain, say, the mountains. The weather is heavy with snow and ice. What do you do to keep from getting lost or in danger? Realize that navigating the outdoors requires a combination of tools and techniques to ensure you stay on course and reach your destination safely. Here are some essential navigation techniques:

Contour Lines
Brown lines represent elevation. Closely spaced contour lines indicate steep terrain. And widely spaced lines indicate gentle slopes.

Elevations
Elevated areas are marked at certain contour lines, typically in meters or feet above sea level.

Colors
Different colors represent different features, such as blue for water bodies, green for vegetation, black for man-made structures, and white for glaciers or rock.

Identifying Key Features

Peaks and Ridges
Peaks and ridges are represented by concentric, closed contour lines with the highest points in the center.

Valleys and Depressions
Valleys and depressions are represented by contour lines forming a U or V shape, with the lowest points in the center.

Saddles
Saddles are areas between two peaks or ridges and are represented by hour-glass-shaped contour lines.

Cliffs and Steep Slopes
Cliffs and slopes are indicated by closely spaced contour lines.

Water Features
Streams, rivers, and lakes are shown in blue.

Trails and Roads
Trails and roads are represented by specific symbols or lines. Roads are often solid lines while trails are usually dotted lines.

Determining Direction and Orientation

North Arrow
The North Arrow, which looks like a black and white triangle with the letter "N" above it, indicates the direction of true north on the map.

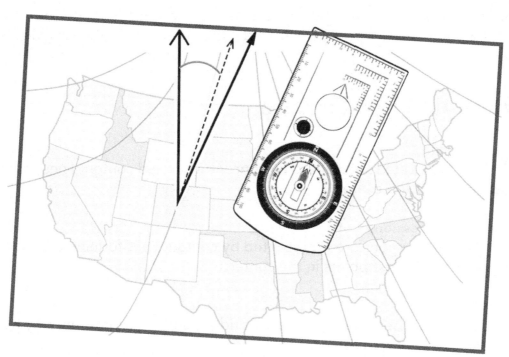

Magnetic Declination
Magnetic declination shows the difference between true north and magnetic north, which is important for using a compass.

Orienting the Map

To properly read the map, align it with the terrain by turning it until the North Arrow points toward true north.

Measuring Distances

Scale

The map scale shows the ratio between distances on the map and actual distances on the ground. The scale bar measures distances directly on the map.

Planning Routes

To plan a designated route, first identify starting and ending points on the

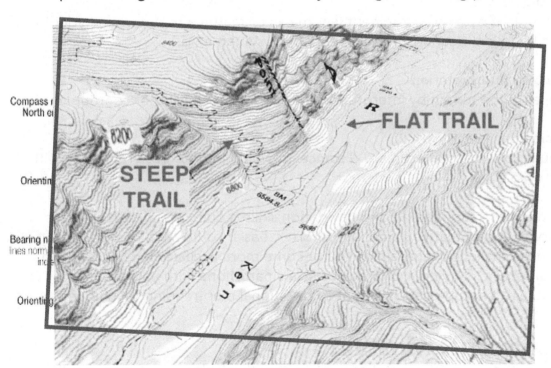

map. Consider terrain features, elevation changes, and potential obstacles or hazards. Plan a route that follows trails, ridges, or contour lines, avoiding steep or dangerous areas. Lastly, estimate travel times based on the distance, terrain, and your hiking pace.

Using a Compass

To properly orient the compass, align its needle with the North Arrow on the map. While keeping the compass oriented, stay along the desired direction of travel and read the bearing from the compass housing. While hiking, periodically check your compass bearing to stay on course.

Terrain Association

Relating the features on the map to the terrain around you is an essential skill for confirming your location and staying oriented. This helps you in identifying distinct landmarks, terrain features, and elevation changes, and matching them to your map.

Additional Techniques

Triangulation

Use triangulation on prominent landmarks or features to determine your location by taking bearings from known points on the map.

Contour Interpretation

Visualize the terrain by interpreting the shape and spacing of contour lines.

Pacing

Count your steps to estimate distances traveled and to cross-reference with the map.

Remember, map-reading and navigation skills require practice. It's always recommended that you start with shorter, easier routes and gradually progress to more challenging terrain as you become more accustomed to travelling. Additionally, carrying a GPS device or a smartphone with navigation apps can serve as a backup or supplement to traditional map-reading techniques.

Compass Navigation

A compass is a fundamental navigation tool that helps you determine directions and follow bearings. Using a compass is an important skill for outdoor navigation and orientation. With time, you can easily master compass use effectively for navigation and triangulation, including adjusting for declination. These next sections will teach you how to properly adjust for magnetic declina

tion, take and follow bearings, and use the compass in conjunction with a map for triangulation:

Understanding the Compass

The compass has a magnetized needle that aligns with the Earth's magnetic field, pointing towards magnetic North. The compass's housing has markings for degrees (0-360°) and cardinal directions (N, S, E, W). The rotating bezel (ring) is used for setting desired bearings or adjusting for declination.

Orienting the Compass

Hold the compass flat in your hand, allowing the needle to settle. Rotate the housing until the "N" (or the red end of the needle) lines up with the orienting arrow or orienting lines in the housing. The compass is now oriented, and the direction of the travel arrow is pointing to the north.

Taking a Bearing

While keeping the compass oriented, rotate the bezel until the desired travel direction lines up with the index pointer or travel arrow. Read the bearing (in degrees) at the index pointer or on the top of the rotating bezel. This bearing represents the direction you will want to travel.

Following a Bearing

While walking, periodically check the compass and adjust your direction to follow the set bearing. Align the travel arrow with the orienting arrow. The red end of the needle should point to the bearing you want to follow.

Adjusting for Declination

Declination is the angle between true north (geographic north pole) and magnetic north. Consult a map or online resource to find the declination value for your area. Adjust the bezel by rotating it clockwise (for easterly declination) or counterclockwise (for westerly declination) by the declination value. This adjustment ensures your bearings align with true north instead of magnetic north.

Triangulation

Triangulation is a method used to determine your position by taking bearings from two or more known landmarks or points on a map. First, identify two or more visible landmarks on the map and take bearings to each one. Next, draw lines on the map from the landmarks, following the bearings you took. Your position is where the lines intersect or form a triangle.

Safety Considerations

Always have a backup plan and carry a map and other navigational tools. Account for potential compass errors or magnetic interference from nearby objects or electrical sources. Practice compass navigation in familiar areas before venturing into unknown terrain. Using a compass effectively requires practice and calibration for your specific area's declination. It's a valuable skill for outdoor adventures, orienteering, and emergency navigation situations. With proper technique and regular use, a compass can be a reliable tool for finding your way through the wilderness.

GPS Navigation

GPS (Global Positioning System) devices can provide accurate location information, track your movements, and guide you along pre-planned routes. Understand how to mark waypoints, follow routes, and integrate GPS in combination with maps and compasses. Using GPS (Global Positioning System) devices can greatly enhance navigation and location finding capabilities. Here's what you should know when it comes to using GPS devices, waypoints, and tracking features for precise navigation:

Understanding GPS

GPS is a satellite-based navigation system that allows devices to determine their precise location, elevation, and time by communicating with a network of satellites orbiting the Earth. GPS devices receive signals from multiple satellites and use trilateration to pinpoint the user's position.

GPS Receivers

Modern GPS receivers come in various forms, including dedicated handheld units, smartphone apps, watches, and integrated systems in vehicles or outdoor gear. Key features to look for include accuracy, battery life, waterproofing, and mapping/navigation capabilities.

Waypoints

Waypoints are sets of coordinates that mark specific locations on a GPS device. You can manually enter waypoint coordinates or mark your current location as a waypoint for future reference. Waypoints are also useful for marking campsites, trailheads, points of interest, or key turns in a route.

Creating and Navigating Routes

Many GPS devices allow you to create and load routes by manually inputting a series of waypoints or by importing pre-planned routes from mapping software or websites. The GPS will provide turn-by-turn navigation instructions to guide you along the planned route, including directions, distances, and estimated times.

Tracking and Recording

GPS devices can record your movements, creating a breadcrumb trail or track log of your route. This feature is useful for retracing your steps, sharing your route with others, or analyzing your journey data after the trip. Some devices allow you to pause and resume tracking or set automatic track logging intervals.

Maps and Mapping Software

Many GPS devices come preloaded with basic maps or allow you to load more detailed topographic maps or aerial imagery. Mapping software like Garmin BaseCamp, Google Earth, or smartphone apps can be used to plan routes, mark waypoints, and transfer data to and from your GPS device.

Coordinates and Datums

GPS devices use different coordinate systems (e.g., latitude/longitude, UTM) and map datums (mathematical models of the Earth's shape) to display locations. Ensure your GPS is set to the correct datum for your area or map to avoid discrepancies between displayed and actual positions.

Best Practices

Always carry backup navigation tools like a compass and paper maps in case of GPS failure or low battery. Clear obstructions for optimal satellite reception, and be aware of potential signal interference in canyons or dense forest. Practice using your GPS device and familiarize yourself with its features before relying on it for critical navigation. GPS technology has revolutionized navigation and location finding, providing unparalleled accuracy and convenience. However, it's essential to understand the basics, limitations, and best practices when using GPS devices to ensure safe and reliable navigation in the outdoors.

Dead Reckoning

Dead reckoning involves estimating your position by keeping track of your

travel direction, distance, and time. Use pacing (counting steps), timing, and compass bearings to continuously update your estimated position on the map.

Route Planning

Before embarking on a journey, carefully plan your route by studying maps, identifying potential hazards or obstacles, and considering factors like elevation gain, terrain difficulty, and water sources. Plan rest stops, campsites, and alternative routes in case of unexpected situations.

Backcountry Navigation

In areas without trails or distinct landmarks, use techniques like terrain contouring (following a specific elevation contour), handrailing (following terrain features like ridgelines or streams), and attack points (aiming for a visible landmark before changing direction).

Contingency Planning

Always have backup plans and contingencies in case of unexpected situations, such as poor weather, injuries, or getting lost. Carry emergency gear, extra

supplies, and communication devices, and know how to signal for help if needed.

Effective navigation requires practice, attention to detail, and a combination of techniques. It's essential to continuously update your location, cross-reference multiple sources of information, and remain vigilant of your surroundings. Additionally, taking a navigation course or joining experienced guides can greatly enhance your outdoor navigation skills.

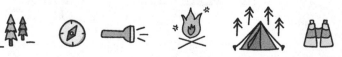

CANNING

  *Book 28*

Book 28:

Canning

Canning has been a regular means of food preservation dating back to France in the late 18th century. It is done by sealing the food in airtight containers and heating it to destroy microorganisms that could cause spoilage. Canning will extend your food's shelf life by several years. To get started, you will need the following equipment:

- Canning jars: Mason jars or other heat-resistant jars with tight-fitting lids and bands.
- Canning pot or water bath canner: A large pot with a rack for water bath canning.
- Pressure canner: A heavy-duty pot with a locking lid and pressure gauge for pressure canning.
- Jar lifter: A tool to safely remove hot jars from the canner.
- Canning utensils: Funnel, bubble remover, lid wand, and jar wrench.
- Supplies: Lids, bands, salt, vinegar, or other canning ingredients.

Water Bath Canning Method

Water bath canning is suitable for high-acid foods like fruits, jams, jellies, pickles, and tomatoes. If you need some guidance on how to start the canning process, follow these guidelines:

- Prepare the jars, lids, and bands by washing the jars with hot water to keep them hot until they're ready to fill. Heat the lids using hot water to soften the rubber gasket. Keep everything hot by continually rinsing with hot water to prevent cracking when filling the jars with hot food. Also remember to use gloves and tongs so you don't get burned.
- Prepare the food according to the recipe instructions. This may involve peeling, chopping, precooking, and adding acid, sugar, or salt.
- Pack the hot food into the hot jars, leaving the recommended headspace at the top (usually 1/4 to 1/2 inch). Run a plastic knife around the insides to remove air bubbles.
- Wipe the jar rims clean with a damp cloth. Place the hot lids on the top of the jars and screw to tighten. Then place bands around the lids and tighten the bands tight enough so your fingertips can't go through them.
- Place the sealed jars into the canner, ensuring they are completely covered with 1-2 inches of hot water.
- Cover the canner and bring the water to a full, rolling boil. Once boiling, set a visible timer for the recommended processing time based on your altitude.
- Once processed, turn off the heat and let the jars sit for 5 more minutes. Carefully remove them from the water and place the jars on a towel to cool for 12-24 hours.
- After cooling, check that the lids have sealed properly by pressing on the lids' center. Any unsealed jars should be refrigerated and used first.

Water Canning Method

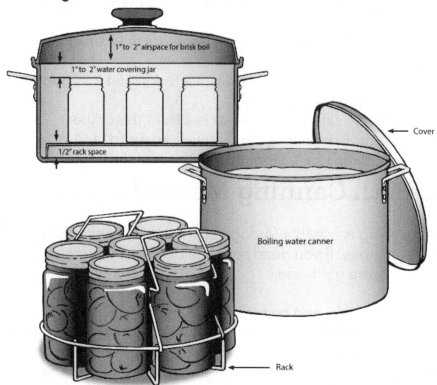

1" to 2" airspace for brisk boil

1" to 2" water covering jar

1/2" rack space

Cover

Boiling water canner

Rack

Pressure Canning Method

- Pressure canning is required for low-acid foods like vegetables, meats, poultry, and seafood to destroy harmful bacteria and spores. The following steps offer a how-to guide for pressure canning:

- Assemble your pressure canner and make sure all vents, gaskets, and other parts are in good working order according to the manufacturer's instructions.

- Prepare your food product following a tested recipe, heating any low-acid foods to at least 180°F prior to packing them into clean, hot jars. Leave the appropriate headspace at the top of the inside of the jar.

- Remove air bubbles by running a plastic utensil between the food and jar. Wipe the rims clean, screw the lids onto the jars, and place bands around the lids. Be sure to tighten the bands fingertip tight.

- Place the jars in the pressure canner on the rack, with jars not touching each other or the canner walls. Add the recommended amount of hot water to the canner.

- Close the canner lid per manufacturer's directions and leave the weight or

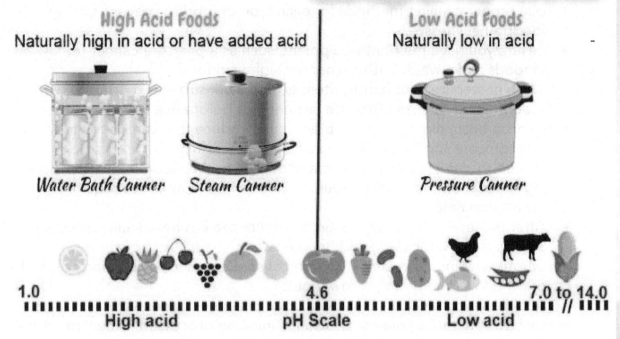

High Acid Foods
Naturally high in acid or have added acid

Low Acid Foods
Naturally low in acid

Water Bath Canner   *Steam Canner*   *Pressure Canner*

1.0   4.6   7.0 to 14.0
High acid   pH Scale   Low acid

petcock off to allow steam venting for 10 minutes.

- After venting, put the weight or petcock on and allow the canner to reach the recommended pressure based on your altitude. Start timing once the desired pressure is reached.
- Adjust heat as needed to maintain constant pressure for the entire timed process listed for that food type and jar size.
- When processing time is complete, remove the canner from the heat and allow pressure to return to zero naturally. Do not force cool the canner.
- Once depressurized, remove the weight or open petcock, and wait 10 more minutes before opening the canner lid away from you.
- Use canner lifters to remove the jars and place them on towels to cool for 12-24 hours. Check the seals once the jars are cool.

Safety Considerations and Practices

Canning allows you to preserve fresh foods for long-term storage when done correctly by following safe guidelines that are up-to-date and scientifically tested. Canning not only preserves the food's freshness but its flavor as well. These foods range from seasonal produce to make shelf-stable meals. It's crucial to follow safe canning practices to ensure the food's quality and safety to prevent spoilage, contamination, and potential foodborne illnesses. Here are some key guidelines and techniques for ensuring safety when canning foods:

- Use proper canning methods for each type of food to prevent spoilage and foodborne illnesses.
- Ensure you have the right equipment, such as a pressure canner for low-acid foods and a water bath canner for high-acid foods.
- Wash or sterilize your hands, utensils, and work surfaces thoroughly with soap or hand sanitizer. Sterilize jars and lids before use as well.
- Choose fresh, high-quality, unblemished produce that can be found at your local grocery and follow recipe instructions carefully.
- Use up-to-date, reliable recipes and adhere to the recommended processing times and pressures for your altitude as higher altitudes require longer processing times.
- After processing, inspect the jars to ensure the lids have sealed properly. Store jars in a cool, dark, and dry place.
- Before opening a jar, check for signs of spoilage, such as bulging lids, leaks, or off-odors. If in doubt, throw it out.
- Avoid canning low-acid foods without a pressure canner. Low-acid foods such as vegetables, meats, and soups must be processed using a pressure canner to prevent botulism.

HOW TO STERILIZE GLASS BOTTLES AND JARS AT HOME

① PLACE THE GLASS JARS AND LIDS
② BRING THE WATER TO A BOIL — 10 min.
③ REMOVE JARS AND CAPS FROM THE POT

- If food is intended to be consumed, consume it within the recommended timeframes.

- Stick to tested recipes and avoid modifying ingredients or processing times, as this can affect food safety.
- Consult reliable sources, such as the USDA or cooperative extension services, for the most up-to-date canning guidelines and safety information.
- By following these precautions, you can minimize the risk of foodborne illnesses and ensure that your home-canned foods are safe to consume.

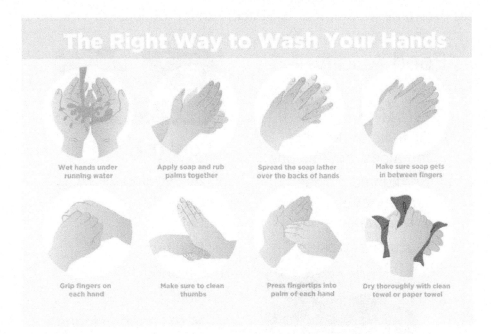

Sterilization and Cleanliness

- Jars, lids, and bands must be sterilized before canning by submerging them in boiling water for at least 10 minutes.
- All equipment, utensils, and work surfaces should be thoroughly cleaned and sanitized with a solution of 1 tablespoon of unscented chlorine bleach per gallon of water.
- Wash your hands frequently with soap and water.
- Use a clean, high-quality canning salt or vinegar.
- Headspace and Sealing
- Leave the recommended amount of headspace (air space at the top of the jar) for expansion during processing and to create a proper vacuum seal.
- After processing, check that lids have properly sealed by pressing on the center - sealed lids will be concave and won't move.
- Remove screw bands after cooling to prevent rusting and allow easier detection of any future seal failures.

Acidity Levels

- Low-acid foods like vegetables, meats, poultry, and seafood must be pressure canned to reach temperatures that destroy harmful bacterial spores.
- High-acid foods like fruits, pickles, and tomatoes can be water bath canned as the acid prevents bacterial growth.
- Add recommended amounts of acid like lemon juice or vinegar to

Food Acidity

High (pH ≤4.6)

- All fruits except figs, tomatoes, and melons
- Fermented pickles (sauerkraut)
- Acidified foods (cucumber pickles)

Low (pH > 4.6)

- All vegetables except rhubarb
- Meats
- Poultry
- Seafood
- Soups
- Mixed canned foods (low-acid + high-acid)

Processing Times

- Precisely follow tested recipes and processing times based on food type, jar size, and altitude.
- Increase processing times by the recommended amount for altitudes above 1,000 feet.
- Under-processing can lead to spoilage from surviving bacteria or mold. Storage and Checking for Spoilage
- Remove rings and wipe down jars before storing to detect any future seal failures.
- Store canned foods in a cool, dark location away from heat sources or moisture.

- Discard any jars with bulging lids, leaks, off odors, or spurting liquid upon opening - signs of spoilage.
- Check periodically and use within recommended timeframes for best quality.

By following proper canning methods, maintaining cleanliness, adjusting for

figure 6 | Measuring Headspace *(Diagram is not to scale)*

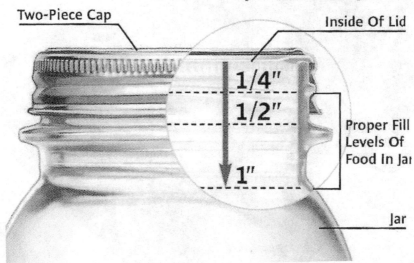

Measure Headspace From The Inside Of
The Lid To The Top Of The Food Or Liquid.

acidity and altitude, and closely adhering to research-tested processing times, you can safely preserve foods at home while preventing spoilage or contamination risks.

Canning Recipes

Here are step-by-step instructions for canning different types of foods:
Canning Fruits
1. Select and wash ripe, fresh fruit. Peel, pit, slice if needed.
2. Pack fruit into clean jars, leaving 1/2 inch headspace. Cover with sugar syrup or fruit juice.
3. Run a plastic spatula around the jar to remove air bubbles.
4. Wipe jar rims clean and place lids/bands on jars.
5. Process in a boiling water bath: Pints for 20-25 mins, Quarts for 25-30 mins.
6. Remove jars and let cool completely before storing.

Gather Your Equipment:
- Canning jars with lids and bands
- Large pot or water bath canner
- Jar lifter
- Funnel
- Ladle
- Towels or rack for cooling

Prepare the Fruit:
- Choose ripe, unblemished fruit.
- Wash, peel (if necessary), pit, and cut the fruit into desired sizes or shapes.
Prepare the Syrup (optional):
- Mix water and sugar in a saucepan, bringing it to a boil until the sugar dissolves.
- The ratio of sugar to water varies depending on desired sweetness.
Sterilize the Jars and Lids:
- Wash the jars, lids, and bands in hot, soapy water and rinse well.
- Place the jars in a large pot or canner, cover with water, and boil for 10 minutes to sterilize.

Fill the Jars:

- Remove the jars from the canner using a jar lifter, pouring out the water.
- Fill the hot jars with prepared fruit using a funnel, leaving 1/2 to 1 inch of headspace.
- If using syrup, pour it over the fruit, maintaining the headspace.
- Remove any air bubbles by running a clean knife or spatula along the inside of the jar.

Seal the Jars:

- Wipe the jar rims with a clean, damp cloth to remove any debris.
- Place the lids and bands on the jars, tightening the bands firmly.

Process the Jars:
- Place the filled jars back into the large pot or canner, ensuring they are covered by at least 1-2 inches of water.
- Bring the water to a boil and process the jars for the recommended time based on the fruit type and jar size (consult a reliable canning guide or recipe).

Cool and Store the Jars:
- Remove the jars from the canner using a jar lifter and place them on a towel or rack to cool.
- Allow the jars to cool for 12-24 hours.

Seal the Jars:

• Wipe the jar rims with a clean, damp cloth to remove any debris.
• Place the lids and bands on the jars, tightening the bands firmly.
Process the Jars:
• Place the filled jars back into the large pot or canner, ensuring they are covered by at least 1-2 inches of water.
• Bring the water to a boil and process the jars for the recommended time based on the fruit type and jar size (consult a reliable canning guide or recipe).

Cool and Store the Jars:

• Remove the jars from the canner using a jar lifter and place them on a towel or rack to cool.
• Allow the jars to cool for 12-24 hours.
• Check the seals by pressing the center of each lid; properly sealed lids should not flex or pop.
• Store sealed jars in a cool, dark place for up to a year.
Remember to always use clean, unblemished jars and fresh lids for canning. Follow a reliable canning guide or recipe for specific processing times and techniques for different fruits. Properly canned fruits can last for several months to a year when stored in a cool, dark place.

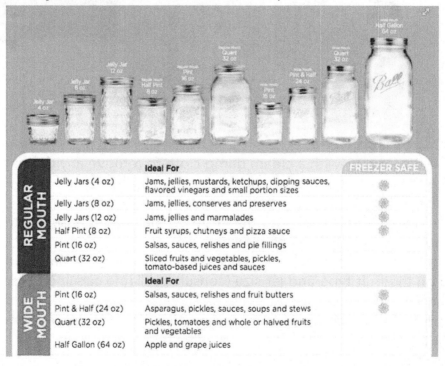

		Ideal For	FREEZER SAFE
REGULAR MOUTH	Jelly Jars (4 oz)	Jams, jellies, mustards, ketchups, dipping sauces, flavored vinegars and small portion sizes	❄
	Jelly Jars (8 oz)	Jams, jellies, conserves and preserves	❄
	Jelly Jars (12 oz)	Jams, jellies and marmalades	❄
	Half Pint (8 oz)	Fruit syrups, chutneys and pizza sauce	❄
	Pint (16 oz)	Salsas, sauces, relishes and pie fillings	
	Quart (32 oz)	Sliced fruits and vegetables, pickles, tomato-based juices and sauces	
		Ideal For	
WIDE MOUTH	Pint (16 oz)	Salsas, sauces, relishes and fruit butters	❄
	Pint & Half (24 oz)	Asparagus, pickles, sauces, soups and stews	❄
	Quart (32 oz)	Pickles, tomatoes and whole or halved fruits and vegetables	
	Half Gallon (64 oz)	Apple and grape juices	

Canning Tomatoes/Tomato Products

- Blanch tomatoes briefly in boiling water to remove skins.
- Pack tomato pieces or crushed tomatoes into jars, leaving 1/2 inch head-space.
- Add 2 Tbsp bottled lemon juice or 1/2 tsp citric acid per quart jar.
- Debubble, wipe rims, add lids/bands.
- Process in a boiling water bath: Pints for 35 mins, Quarts for 45 mins.

Gather Your Equipment:
- Water bath canner or large pot with a rack
- Canning jars with lids and bands
- Jar lifter
- Funnel
- Ladle
- Towels or rack for cooling

Prepare the Tomatoes:
- Choose ripe, unblemished tomatoes.
- Wash the tomatoes and remove any stems or cores.
- Cut an X in the bottom of each tomato to facilitate peeling.

Blanch and Peel the Tomatoes:
- Bring a large pot of water to a boil.
- Submerge the tomatoes in the boiling water for 30-60 seconds, then immediately transfer them to a bowl of ice water.
- Once cooled, peel the skins off the tomatoes.
- Sterilize the Jars and Lids:
- Wash the jars, lids, and bands in hot, soapy water and rinse well.
- Place the jars in the canner or pot, cover with water, and boil for 10 minutes to sterilize.

- Simmer the lids and bands in a separate pot for 5 minutes.

Fill the Jars:
- Remove the jars from the canner using a jar lifter, pouring out the water.
- Fill the hot jars with peeled tomatoes, leaving 1/2 inch of headspace.
- Add 1 tablespoon of bottled lemon juice or 1/4 teaspoon of citric acid to each pint jar (double the amounts for quart jars) to ensure acidity.
- If desired, add 1/2 teaspoon of salt per pint jar (1 teaspoon for quart jars).

Seal the Jars:
- Wipe the jar rims with a clean, damp cloth to remove any debris.
- Place the lids and bands on the jars, tightening the bands firmly.

Process the Jars:

- Place the filled jars into the canner or pot, ensuring they are covered by at least 1-2 inches of water.
- Bring the water to a boil and process the jars for the recommended time based on your altitude and jar size (consult a reliable canning guide or recipe).
- Cool and Store the Jars:
- Remove the jars from the canner using a jar lifter and place them on a towel or rack to cool.
- Allow the jars to cool for 12-24 hours.

- Check the seals by pressing the center of each lid; properly sealed lids should not flex or pop.
- Store sealed jars in a cool, dark place for up to a year.

Always use clean, unblemished jars and fresh lids for canning. Follow a reliable canning guide or recipe for specific processing times and techniques. Properly canned tomatoes can last for several months to a year when stored in a cool, dark place.

Canning Vegetables

1. Prepare vegetables - wash, peel, slice etc.

2. Pack hot into clean jars, leaving 1 inch headspace. Add hot cooking liquid if desired.
3. Debubble, wipe rims, add lids and bands.
4. Process in a pressure canner at appropriate pressure for your altitude.

Processing times vary by vegetable and size, e.g. 25-30 mins for pints of green beans.

Gather your Equipment:
- Pressure canner
- Canning jars with lids and bands
- Jar lifter
- Funnel
- Ladle
- Towels or rack for cooling

Prepare the Vegetables:
- Choose fresh, firm vegetables.
- Wash, trim, and cut the vegetables into desired sizes or shapes.
Sterilize the Jars and Lids:

Fill the Jars:
- Remove the jars from the canner using a jar lifter, pouring out the water.
- Pack the vegetables into the hot jars using a funnel, leaving 1 inch of head-space.
- Pour boiling water or brine (if called for in the recipe) over the vegetables, maintaining the headspace.
- Remove any air bubbles by running a clean knife or spatula along the inside of the jar.

Seal the Jars:
- Wipe the jar rims with a clean, damp cloth to remove any debris.
- Place the lids and bands on the jars, tightening the bands firmly.

Process the Jars:
- Place the filled jars into the pressure canner, following the manufacturer's instructions for proper placement and water level.
- Close and lock the canner lid, allowing it to vent steam for the specified time (usually 10 minutes).
- Place the pressure regulator on the vent and process the jars at the recommended pressure and time based on the vegetable type and jar size (consult a reliable canning guide or recipe).

Cool and Store the Jars:
- After processing, allow the canner to cool and depressurize naturally.
- Remove the jars from the canner using a jar lifter and place them on a towel or rack to cool.
- Allow the jars to cool for 12-24 hours.
- Check the seals by pressing the center of each lid; properly sealed lids should not flex or pop.
- Store sealed jars in a cool, dark place for up to a year.

It's crucial to use a pressure canner when canning vegetables, as the high temperatures achieved during pressure canning are necessary to eliminate the risk of botulism. Always follow a reliable canning guide or recipe for specific processing times, pressures, and techniques for different vegetables. Properly canned vegetables can last for several months to a year when stored in a cool, dark place.

Canning Meats
1. Prep meat/seafood by removing bones, fat, skin as desired. Cut into chunks or strips.
2. Pack hot meat into jars, leaving 1 inch headspace. Add hot meat broth or water.
3. Debubble, wipe rims, add lids/bands.
4. Process in a pressure canner, following recommended times e.g. 75 mins for quarts of chicken/beef.

Canning meat requires careful attention to safety and proper processing techniques.

Gather your Equipment:
- Pressure canner
- Canning jars with lids and bands
- Jar lifter
- Funnel
- Ladle
- Towels or rack for cooling

Prepare the Meat:
- Choose fresh, high-quality meat.

- Trim away excess fat and cut the meat into desired sizes or cubes.

Brown the Meat (optional):
- If desired, brown the meat in a skillet or oven to enhance flavor and appearance.

Pack the Jars:
- Sterilize the jars and lids by boiling them in water for 10 minutes.
- Pack the meat into the hot jars, leaving 1 inch of headspace.

- Add salt if desired (1/2 teaspoon per pint jar or 1 teaspoon per quart jar).

Add Liquid:
- Pour boiling water, broth, or tomato juice over the meat, maintaining the 1-inch headspace.
- Remove any air bubbles by running a clean knife or spatula along the inside of the jar.

Seal the Jars:
- Wipe the jar rims with a clean, damp cloth to remove any debris.
- Place the lids and bands on the jars, tightening the bands firmly.

Process the Jars:
- Place the filled jars into the pressure canner, following the manufacturer's instructions for proper placement and water level.
- Close and lock the canner lid, allowing it to vent steam for the specified time (usually 10 minutes).

- Close and lock the canner lid, allowing it to vent steam for the specified time (usually 10 minutes).
- Place the pressure regulator on the vent and process the jars at the recommended pressure and time based on the type of meat and jar size (consult a reliable canning guide or recipe).

Cool and Store the Jars:
- After processing, allow the canner to cool and depressurize naturally.
- Remove the jars from the canner using a jar lifter and place them on a towel or rack to cool.
- Allow the jars to cool for 12-24 hours.
- Check the seals by pressing the center of each lid; properly sealed lids should not flex or pop.
- Store sealed jars in a cool, dark place for up to a year.

It's essential to use a pressure canner when canning meat, as the high temperatures achieved during pressure canning are necessary to eliminate the risk of botulism. Always follow a reliable canning guide or recipe for specific processing times, pressures, and techniques for different types of meat. Properly canned meat can last for several months to a year when stored in a cool, dark place.

Canning Poultry

Canning poultry, such as chicken or turkey, requires precise techniques to ensure safe preservation. Here's a step-by-step guide on how to can poultry:

Gather your Equipment:
- Pressure canner
- Canning jars with lids and bands
- Jar lifter
- Funnel
- Ladle
- Towels or rack for cooling

Prepare the Poultry:
- Choose fresh, high-quality poultry.
- Remove skin, bones, and excess fat.
- Cut the meat into desired sizes or cubes.

Pack the Jars:
- Sterilize the jars and lids by boiling them in water for 10 minutes.

- Pack the meat into the hot jars, leaving 1 inch of headspace.
- Add salt if desired (1/2 teaspoon per pint jar or 1 teaspoon per quart jar).

Add Liquid:
- Pour boiling water, broth, or tomato juice over the meat, maintaining the 1-inch headspace.
- Remove any air bubbles by running a clean knife or spatula along the inside of the jar.

Seal the Jars:
- Wipe the jar rims with a clean, damp cloth to remove any debris.
- Place the lids and bands on the jars, tightening the bands firmly.
Process the Jars:
- Place the filled jars into the pressure canner, following the manufacturer's instructions for proper placement and water level.
- Close and lock the canner lid, allowing it to vent steam for the specified time (usually 10 minutes).
- Place the pressure regulator on the vent and process the jars at the recommended pressure and time based on the type of meat and jar size (consult a reliable canning guide or recipe).

Cool and Store the Jars:
- After processing, allow the canner to cool and depressurize naturally.
- Remove the jars from the canner using a jar lifter and place them on a towel or rack to cool.
- Allow the jars to cool for 12-24 hours.
- Check the seals by pressing the center of each lid; properly sealed lids should not flex or pop.
- Store sealed jars in a cool, dark place for up to a year.

It's essential to use a pressure canner when canning meat, as the high temperatures achieved during pressure canning are necessary to eliminate the risk of botulism. Always follow a reliable canning guide or recipe for specific processing times, pressures, and techniques for different types of meat. Properly canned meat can last for several months to a year when stored in a cool, dark place.

   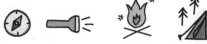

Canning Poultry

Canning poultry, such as chicken or turkey, requires precise techniques to ensure safe preservation. Here's a step-by-step guide on how to can poultry:

Gather your Equipment:
- Pressure canner
- Canning jars with lids and bands
- Jar lifter
- Funnel
- Ladle
- Towels or rack for cooling

Prepare the Poultry:
- Choose fresh, high-quality poultry.
- Remove skin, bones, and excess fat.
- Cut the meat into desired sizes or cubes.

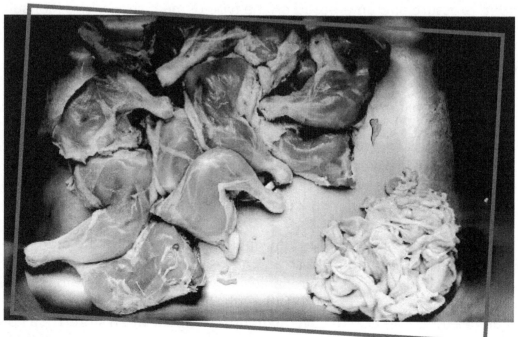

Pack the Jars:
- Sterilize the jars and lids by boiling them in water for 10 minutes.
- Pack the poultry into the hot jars, leaving 1 1/4 inch of headspace.

- Remove any air bubbles by running a clean knife or spatula along the inside of the jar.

Seal the Jars:
- Wipe the jar rims with a clean, damp cloth to remove any debris.
- Place the lids and bands on the jars, tightening the bands firmly.

Process the Jars:
- Place the filled jars into the pressure canner, following the manufacturer's instructions for proper placement and water level.

- Close and lock the canner lid, allowing it to vent steam for the specified time (usually 10 minutes).
- Place the pressure regulator on the vent and process the jars at the recommended pressure and time based on your altitude and jar size (consult a reliable canning guide or recipe).

Cool and Store the Jars:
- After processing, allow the canner to cool and depressurize naturally.
- Remove the jars from the canner using a jar lifter and place them on a towel or rack to cool.
- Allow the jars to cool for 12-24 hours.
- Check the seals by pressing the center of each lid; properly sealed lids

flex or pop.

• Store sealed jars in a cool, dark place for up to a year.

It's crucial to use a pressure canner when canning poultry, as the high temperatures achieved during pressure canning are necessary to eliminate the risk of botulism. Always follow a reliable canning guide or recipe for specific processing times, pressures, and techniques. Properly canned poultry can last for several months to a year when stored in a cool, dark place.

Note: If you prefer bone-in poultry, you can follow the same process but adjust the processing time accordingly, as bone-in poultry may require longer processing.

Canning Seafood

Canning seafood requires precise techniques to ensure safe preservation. Here's a step-by-step guide on how to can seafood:

Gather your Equipment:
• Pressure canner

- Canning jars with lids and bands
- Jar lifter
- Funnel
- Ladle
- Towels or rack for cooling

Prepare the Seafood:
- Choose fresh, high-quality seafood.
- Clean, rinse, and remove any shells, heads, or tails as needed.

- Cut larger fish into suitable sizes for jars.

Pack the Jars:
- Sterilize the jars and lids by boiling them in water for 10 minutes.
- Pack the seafood into the hot jars, leaving 1 inch of headspace.
- Add salt if desired (1/2 teaspoon per pint jar or 1 teaspoon per quart jar).

Add Liquid:
- For fish, you can add water, tomato juice, or oil.
- For clams or mussels, use the liquid from cooking them.
- Maintain the 1-inch headspace and remove any air bubbles.
Seal the Jars:
- Wipe the jar rims with a clean, damp cloth to remove any debris.

- Place the lids and bands on the jars, tightening the bands firmly.

Process the jars:
- Place the filled jars into the pressure canner, following the manufacturer's instructions for proper placement and water level.
- Close and lock the canner lid, allowing it to vent steam for the specified time (usually 10 minutes).
- Place the pressure regulator on the vent and process the jars at the recommended pressure and time based on the type of seafood, jar size, and your altitude (consult a reliable canning guide or recipe).

Cool and Store the Jars:
- After processing, allow the canner to cool and depressurize naturally.
- Remove the jars from the canner using a jar lifter and place them on a towel or rack to cool.
- Allow the jars to cool for 12-24 hours.
- Check the seals by pressing the center of each lid; properly sealed lids should not flex or pop.
- Store sealed jars in a cool, dark place for up to a year.

It's essential to use a pressure canner when canning seafood, as the high temperatures achieved during pressure canning are necessary to eliminate the risk of botulism. Always follow a reliable canning guide or recipe for specific processing times, pressures, and techniques for different types of seafood. Properly canned seafood can last for several months to a year when stored in a cool, dark place.

Note: Some types of seafood, such as smoked fish or fish in oil, may require different processing methods. Always consult a reliable canning resource for specific instructions on canning various types of seafood.

Canning Soups/Stews/Broth
1. Prepare soup/stew, cooking ingredients until ready.
2. Reheat mixture, then pack hot into jars, leaving 1 inch headspace.
3. Debubble, add lids/bands.

Process soups/stews in a pressure canner, following times for meat/veg ingredients. For broth, process at 20 mins for pints, 25 mins for quarts.
Always use reliable, scientifically-tested recipes and processing times. Adjust as needed for altitude. Let the jars cool undisturbed before removing any rings

and checking the seals.

Gather your Equipment:
- Pressure canner
- Canning jars with lids and bands
- Jar lifter
- Funnel
- Ladle
- Towels or rack for cooling

Prepare the Soup, Stew, or Broth:
- Make your soup, stew, or broth recipe as usual, but avoid using ingredients that don't can well, such as noodles or dairy products.
- Simmer the soup, stew, or broth to cook all ingredients thoroughly.

Sterilize the Jars and Lids:
- Wash the jars, lids, and bands in hot, soapy water and rinse well.
- Place the jars in the pressure canner, cover with water, and boil for 10 minutes to sterilize.
- Simmer the lids and bands in a separate pot for 5 minutes.

Fill the Jars:
- Remove the hot jars from the canner using a jar lifter.
- Ladle the hot soup, stew, or broth into the jars, leaving 1 inch of headspace.
- Remove any air bubbles by running a clean knife or spatula along the inside of the jar.

Seal the Jars:
- Wipe the jar rims with a clean, damp cloth to remove any debris.
- Place the lids and bands on the jars, tightening the bands firmly.

Process the Jars:
- Place the filled jars into the pressure canner, following the manufacturer's instructions for proper placement and water level.
- Close and lock the canner lid, allowing it to vent steam for the specified time (usually 10 minutes).
- Place the pressure regulator on the vent and process the jars at the recommended pressure and time based on your altitude ad jar size (consult a reliable canning guide or recipe).

Cool and Store the Jars:
- After processing, allow the canner to cool and depressurize naturally.
- Remove the jars from the canner using a jar lifter and place them on a towel

or rack to cool.
- Allow the jars to cool for 12-24 hours.
- Check the seals by pressing the center of each lid; properly sealed lids should not flex or pop.
- Store sealed jars in a cool, dark place for up to a year.

It's crucial to use a pressure canner when canning soups, stews and/or broth, as the high temperatures achieved during pressure canning are necessary to eliminate the risk of botulism. Always follow a reliable canning guide or recipe for specific processing times, pressures, and techniques. Properly canned soups, stews, and broth can last for several months to a year when stored in a cool, dark place.

RADIO/HAM COMMUNICATION

  **Book 29**

Radio communication involves the transmission and reception of signals using radio waves, which are a type of electromagnetic radiation. Here are the fundamentals of radio communication, including terminology, frequencies, and modulation types:

Terminology

- Transmitter: A device that generates and sends radio signals.
- Receiver: A device that receives and demodulates radio signals.
- Antenna: A device that converts electrical signals into radio waves (for transmission) or radio waves into electrical signals (for reception).
- Frequency: The number of cycles or oscillations per second, measured in Hertz (Hz).
- Wavelength: The distance between two consecutive peaks or troughs in a wave, inversely proportional to the frequency.
- Bandwidth: The range of frequencies required for transmitting a signal.

Radio Frequency Spectrum

Radio waves span a wide range of frequencies, from extremely low frequen

Radio Frequency Spectrum: Ranges

Designation	Abbreviation	Frequencies	Wavelengths
Very Low Frequency	VLF	3 kHz - 30 kHz	100 km - 10 km
Low Frequency	LF	30 kHz - 300 kHz	10 km - 1 km
Medium Frequency	MF	300 kHz - 3 MHz	1 km - 100 m
High Frequency	HF	3 MHz - 30 MHz	100 m - 10 m
Very High Frequency	VHF	30 MHz - 300 MHz	10 m - 1 m
Ultra High Frequency	UHF	300 MHz - 3 GHz	1 m - 100 mm
Super High Frequency	SHF	3 GHz - 30 GHz	100 mm - 10 mm
Extremely High Frequency	EHF	30 GHz - 300 GHz	10 mm - 1 mm

cies (ELF) to extremely high frequencies (EHF). Different frequency bands are allocated for various applications, such as AM/FM radio, television, mobile communications, satellite communications, and more.

Common frequency bands include:

High Frequency (HF)
3 MHz to 30 MHz (used for shortwave radio)

Very High Frequency (VHF)
30 MHz to 300 MHz (used for FM radio, television, and two-way radios)

Ultra-High Frequency (UHF)
300 MHz to 3 GHz (used for television, cellular networks, and Wi-Fi)

Modulation Types
Modulation is the process of encoding information onto a radio wave carrier signal. You may be familiar with some modulation types as you listen to the radio in your vehicle or at home when listening to music (usually FM) or talk radio (usually AM).

Amplitude Modulation (AM)
The amplitude (strength) of the carrier wave is varied according to the information signal.

Frequency Modulation (FM)
The frequency of the carrier wave is varied according to the information signal.

Phase Modulation (PM)
The phase of the carrier wave is varied according to the information signal.

Digital Modulation
Digital data is encoded onto the carrier wave using techniques like Phase-Shift Keying (PSK), Frequency-Shift Keying (FSK), or Quadrature Amplitude Modulation (QAM).

Radio Communication Systems
Radio communication systems can be simplex (one-way communication), half-duplex (two-way communication, but not simultaneous), or full-duplex (simultaneous two-way communication).

Common radio communication systems include:
- Broadcast radio (AM, FM)

- Broadcast radio (AM, FM)
- Two-way radio (walkie-talkies, citizen's band (CB) radio)
- Mobile radio (cellular networks, public safety communications)
- Satellite communications
- Wireless computer networks (Wi-Fi, Bluetooth)

Regulations and Licensing

Radio communication is regulated by government agencies, such as the Federal Communications Commission (FCC) in the United States, to ensure efficient use of the radio spectrum and prevent interference. Certain radio services and frequency bands require licenses or certifications for operation.

Understanding the fundamentals of radio communication, including terminology, frequencies, modulation types, and communication systems, is essential for working with various radio technologies and applications, such as broadcasting, wireless communications, and radio-based navigation.

- Transmitters generate and send radio frequency (RF) signals
- Receivers detect and demodulate RF signals into usable information
- Antennas convert electrical signals to electromagnetic radio waves

The Role of FCC in Ensuring Public Safety

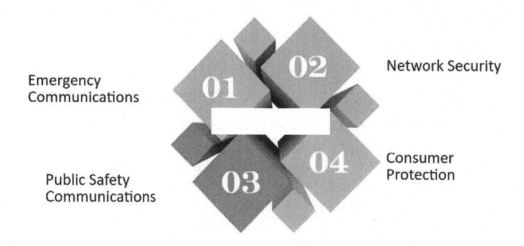

Emergency Communications — 01
02 — Network Security
Public Safety Communications — 03
04 — Consumer Protection

- RF signals are classified by frequency ranges (HF, VHF, UHF, etc.)
- Modulation encodes information onto a carrier wave (AM, FM, digital)

Operating Modes
- Voice: Single Sideband (SSB) for HF, FM for VHF/UHF
- Digital: RTTY, PSK for keyboard communications
- CW (Morse code) at higher HF frequencies
- Satellite communications via amateur radio satellites

Ham Radio

Ham radio is an amateur radio service for non-commercial exchange of messages and technical experimentation. It requires a license from governing agencies (FCC in the US) to legally operate and multiple license classes (Technician, General, Amateur Extra) grant operating privileges. Ham radio uses designated frequency bands allocated for amateur radio use. Common ham radio activities include: voice/digital communications, emergency communications, contesting, and radio construction.

Ham Radio Equipment
- Handheld transceivers for VHF/UHF bands - good for local communications
- Mobile transceivers installed in vehicles
- Base station radios are more powerful units installed at a fixed location
- Antenna systems matched to desired frequency/application (dipoles, yagis, vertical, etc.)

Using Ham Radio Equipment
Using ham radio equipment involves several steps and requires a basic understanding of radio communication principles and regulations. Here's a general guide on how to use ham radio equipment:
- Obtain a license: In most countries, operating a ham radio requires a license. Study for and pass the appropriate license exam for your country or region.
- Acquire equipment: Purchase a ham radio transceiver suitable for your license class and operating interests. Consider additional equipment such as antennas, power supplies, and microphones.
- Familiarize yourself with the equipment: Read the manual and understand the functions of your transceiver. Learn how to adjust settings such as frequency, mode, power output, and squelch.
- Connect your equipment: Connect your antenna to the transceiver using the appropriate cable and connectors. Connect the power supply to the transceiver, ensuring proper voltage and polarity.
- Determine your operating frequency: Consult a band plan or frequency chart

- Determine your operating frequency: Consult a band plan or frequency chart for the frequencies allocated to your license class. Choose an appropriate frequency for your desired communication mode (e.g., voice, digital, or Morse code).
- Operate your transceiver: Power on your transceiver and set the frequency and mode. Use the microphone or keys to transmit and listen for responses using the speaker or headphones. Follow proper operating procedures, such as identifying your station and avoiding interference with other users.
- Learn and use proper etiquette: Use the International Telecommunication Union (ITU) phonetic alphabet to spell out words or callsigns. Keep transmissions brief and allow time for others to respond. Avoid transmitting on top of other stations and wait for a clear frequency before calling.
- Experiment with different modes and activities: Try communicating using voice, digital modes, or Morse code. Participate in contests, special events, or emergency communication exercises to improve your skills and contribute to the ham radio community.
- Maintain your equipment: Regularly inspect and maintain your antenna, cables, and connectors. Keep your transceiver clean and protected from dust, moisture, and extreme temperatures.

Remember, ham radio operation is regulated by national and international laws. Always follow the rules and regulations set forth by your local government and the International Amateur Radio Union (IARU). Proper use of ham radio equipment involves not only technical skills but also a commitment to responsible and ethical operation.

Ham Radio Activities
- Rag chewing - informal conversation between amateur radio operators
- Emergency communications support during disasters (ARES/RACES)
- Radio contesting and awards for making contacts globally
- Building and experimenting with radio equipment
- Radio direction finding (transmitter hunting)

As a hobby, amateur radio encourages technical self-training, emergency preparedness, and international goodwill. Proper licensing and adherence to regulations is required for legal ham radio operation.

Ham Radio Licensing
Obtaining a HAM radio license is a great way to get started in the exciting world

of amateur radio. Here's some guidance on the licensing process, study resources, and exam preparation tips:

Licensing Levels

In the United States, there are three levels of amateur radio licenses issued by the Federal Communications Commission (FCC):

• Technician Class: This entry-level license allows you to operate on all VHF and UHF amateur bands, as well as some limited HF privileges.
• General Class: With this license, you gain full privileges on the HF bands, allowing you to communicate worldwide.
• Amateur Extra Class: The highest level, granting all available amateur radio privileges, including access to exclusive frequency bands.

Study Resources

• License Manuals: Look for study guides specific to the license level you're pursuing. Popular options include the ARRL (American Radio Relay League) license manuals and the Gordon West books.
• Online Practice Tests: Websites like QRZ.com, HamStudy.org, and AA9PW.com offer free online practice tests for each license level.
• Local Ham Radio Clubs: Many clubs offer licensing classes and study groups,

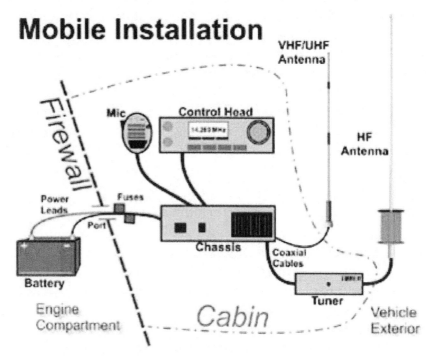

Mobile Installation

providing hands-on guidance and support.
• YouTube Videos: Search for video tutorials and explanations on topics covered in the license exams.

Exam Preparation Tips
• Set a Study Schedule: Dedicate regular time for studying and reviewing the material, especially the more technical concepts.
• Take Practice Exams: Regularly take practice tests to identify your weak areas and focus your study efforts.
• Join a Study Group: Studying with others can help reinforce concepts and provide motivation.
• Understand the Concepts: Don't just memorize answers; aim to understand the underlying principles and theories.
• Learn with Hands-on Activities: Build simple circuits or experiment with radios to solidify your understanding.
• Stay Organized: Use flashcards, notes, or study guides to organize the material effectively.
• Get Plenty of Rest: Ensure you're well-rested before the exam to improve focus and recall.

The exams are multiple-choice, and you'll need to achieve a passing score of 74% for the Technician and 65% for the General and Extra Class licenses. Once you pass, your license is valid for 10 years and can be renewed by passing the corresponding exam again or upgrading to a higher license level.
With dedication and proper preparation, obtaining a HAM radio license is an achievable goal that opens up a world of experimentation, communication, and community.

Emergency Communication Protocols
Effective communication during emergencies is crucial for coordinating response efforts, relaying important information, and ensuring the safety of those involved. Here are some protocols and procedures for communicating during emergencies, including the use of emergency frequencies and radio codes:

Emergency Frequencies
Emergency services and agencies have dedicated radio frequencies for communication during emergencies. In the United States, common emergency frequencies include the National Emergency Channels (158.7375 MHz and

159.4725 MHz) and the VHF High band (155.7625 MHz and 154.4275 MHz). These frequencies are monitored by emergency responders and should be used only for actual emergencies or communication with authorized personnel.

Radio Codes and Procedures

Radio codes and procedures help maintain clear, concise, and standardized communication during emergencies. Common radio codes include:

- 10-codes (e.g., 10-4 for "Affirmative" or 10-20 for "Location")
- Phonetic alphabet (Alpha, Bravo, Charlie, etc.) for spelling out words or call-signs
- Prowords (e.g., "Over" to indicate the end of a transmission, "Roger" for acknowledgment)

Follow proper radio etiquette, such as using clear speech, avoiding unnecessary chatter, and listening before transmitting to prevent interference.

Incident Command System (ICS)

The ICS is a standardized management system used by emergency responders to coordinate operations during incidents or emergencies. Communication protocols within the ICS include the use of clear text (avoiding codes or jargon) and following a chain of command for relaying information and requests.

Emergency Communication Plans

Organizations and agencies should have pre-established emergency communication plans that outline protocols, frequencies, and procedures for different types of emergencies. These plans should be regularly reviewed, updated, and practiced through drills or exercises.

Backup Communication Methods

In addition to radio communication, it's essential to have backup methods in case primary systems fail or become overwhelmed. Backup methods may include satellite phones, amateur radio networks (ARES/RACES), or dedicated emergency communication systems.

Information Management

During emergencies, it's crucial to manage and relay accurate and timely information to the appropriate personnel or agencies. Establish procedures for verifying information, prioritizing transmissions, and documenting communications for record-keeping and future analysis.

Interoperability

Emergency responders from different agencies or jurisdictions may need to communicate with each other during large-scale emergencies. Ensure interoperability by establishing common communication protocols, frequencies, and procedures that all parties can follow.

Effective emergency communication requires training, practice, and adherence to established protocols and procedures. Clear and concise communication can help minimize confusion, improve coordination, and ultimately save lives during emergencies.

VEHICLE PREPAREDNESS & MAINTENANCE

  **Book 30**

When you own a car, truck, SUV, van, or even a motorcycle, you will need to take good care of it to ensure that it lasts a long time. If you are not familiar with the essential vehicle maintenance procedures, you can learn them by reading your owner's manual that comes in your glove compartment. To keep your vehicle in tip-top shape, you need to carefully assess certain car features like the brakes, head and taillights, and windshield wipers and how they function. These features will be expounded upon further in this book.

Basic Vehicle Maintenance

Regular maintenance is essential for keeping your vehicle in optimal condition and ensuring safe and reliable operation. Here are some important maintenance tasks you should perform regularly:

Fluid Checks

Fluid is what keeps your vehicle running consistently. If the fluids in your vehicle are not cared for or changed when they need to be, you will no longer be able to use your vehicle. Performing a fluid check is an essential part of vehicle maintenance. Here's a general guide on how to check the main fluids in your vehicle:

Engine Oil

Checking your car's engine oil is a simple process that should be done regularly to maintain your vehicle's health. If the oil level is low, you will have to change the oil and filter according to the manufacturer's recommended intervals or every 5,000-7,500 miles (8,000-12,000 km). Here's a step-by-step guide:

- Park your car on a level surface and turn off the engine. Wait a few minutes for the oil to settle back into the oil pan.
- Open the hood and locate the oil dipstick. It usually has a brightly colored handle (often yellow or orange) and is located near the engine.
- Pull the dipstick out and wipe it clean with a lint-free cloth or paper towel.
- Reinsert the dipstick fully back into its tube, then pull it out again.
- Check the oil level and color: The oil level should be between the two marks on the dipstick (usually labeled as "low" and "full" or with "L" and "F"). If the level is below the minimum mark, you need to add oil. The oil color should be light brown to black. If it appears milky or grayish, or if you see metal particles, contact a mechanic.

- If the oil level is low, add the recommended oil for your vehicle (check your owner's manual). Use a funnel to pour the oil into the oil filler cap opening, which is usually located on top of the engine.
- Wait a minute for the oil to settle, then recheck the level using the dipstick. Be careful not to overfill, as this can cause engine damage.
- Once the level is correct, replace the dipstick and close the oil filler cap securely.
- Close the hood.

Regularly checking and maintaining the proper oil level helps keep your engine lubricated and running smoothly. Consult your owner's manual for the recommended oil change intervals and oil type for your specific vehicle.

Coolant

Check the coolant level in the overflow reservoir and top it up if needed. Flush and replace the coolant at recommended intervals. Your car's coolant level is an important part of vehicle maintenance. Always check the coolant level when the engine is cold to avoid burning from hot coolant or steam. Here's how to do it:

- Park your car on a level surface and ensure the engine is cold.
- Open the hood and locate the coolant reservoir. It's usually a translucent plastic tank near the radiator, with level markings on the side.
- Check the coolant level visually. The coolant should be between the "low" and "full" marks on the reservoir. If the reservoir is opaque, you may need to remove the cap to check the level.
- If the coolant level is below the "low" mark, you'll need to add more coolant.
- Before adding coolant, check the owner's manual for the recommended type of coolant for your vehicle. Use a 50/50 mix of concentrated coolant and distilled water or use pre-mixed coolant.
- If necessary, remove the reservoir cap carefully. Place a rag over the cap and slowly turn it to release any pressure.
- Add the coolant mixture until it reaches the "full" mark on the reservoir. Do not overfill, as this can cause leaks or overflow.
- Replace the cap securely and close the hood.
- Start the engine and let it run for a few minutes. Check for any leaks around the reservoir or radiator.

If you notice that your coolant level is consistently low or find a leak, have your vehicle inspected by a professional mechanic. Always consult your vehicle's owner's manual for specific instructions and safety precautions related to your make and model.

Brake Fluid

The brake fluid level in the reservoir will need to be inspected as well. Replacing your car's brake fluid is an essential part of vehicle maintenance.

You will need to top it up if it's low. Brake fluid should be replaced every 2-3 years or as recommended by the manufacturer. Here's a general guide on how to replace your car's brake fluid:

• Gather the necessary materials including brake fluid (as specified by your vehicle's manual), a clean turkey baster or brake fluid syringe, a container for waste fluid, and clean rags.
• Locate the brake fluid reservoir, which is usually found near the back of the engine compartment.
• Clean the reservoir and surrounding area with a rag to prevent dirt from entering the system.
• Remove the reservoir cap and check the current fluid level and color. If it's dark or contaminated, the fluid will need to be replaced.

• Refill the reservoir with fresh brake fluid up to the "MAX" line. Be careful not to spill any fluid, as it can damage your vehicle's paint.

• Locate the brake bleeder valves on each wheel caliper. Start with the caliper farthest from the reservoir (usually the right rear).

• Have an assistant pump the brake pedal several times, then hold it down.

• While the pedal is held down, open the bleeder valve slightly to allow the old fluid to escape. Close the valve before the pedal reaches the floor.

• Repeat steps 8-9 until fresh, clean fluid appears at the bleeder valve. Then, close the valve and move on to the next caliper.

• Monitor the fluid level in the reservoir and top it off as needed to prevent air from entering the system.

• After bleeding all four calipers, pump the brake pedal to ensure it feels firm and not spongy.

• Replace the reservoir cap and clean up any spills.

Brake fluid replacement can be tricky, and if done incorrectly, it can compromise your vehicle's braking system. If you're unsure about the process, it's best to have the job done by a professional mechanic. Always consult your vehicle's owner's manual for specific instructions and safety precautions.

Transmission Fluid

The transmission fluid level and its condition will also need a regular maintenance check-up. Make sure to change the transmission fluid according to the manufacturer's recommendations. The process can vary depending on whether your car has a dipstick or not, and if it has automatic or manual transmission. Here's a general guide on transmission fluid replacement:

For vehicles with a dipstick (mostly older vehicles):

• Park your car on a level surface and start the engine. Let it run until it reaches normal operating temperature.

• Locate the transmission dipstick (consult your owner's manual if needed). It's usually found near the back of the engine compartment, and it may have a red or yellow handle.

• With the engine running and the transmission in "Park" (or "Neutral" for manual transmissions), pull out the dipstick, wipe it clean with a lint-free cloth, reinsert it fully, and pull it out again.

• Check the fluid level. It should be between the "Low" and "Full" marks on the dipstick. The color should be bright red to light brown. If it's dark or smells burnt, it may need to be changed.

• If the level is low, add the recommended transmission fluid in small increments, rechecking the level each time to avoid overfilling.

For vehicles without a dipstick (mostly newer vehicles):

• Most modern vehicles have sealed transmissions without dipsticks. Checking the fluid level in these cases often requires special tools and procedures.

• Consult your vehicle's owner's manual for specific instructions on checking the transmission fluid level. Some may require the vehicle to be at a certain temperature and on level ground.

• If you're unsure about the process or don't have the necessary tools, it's best to have the fluid level checked by a professional mechanic.

Note: For some vehicles, the transmission fluid level can only be checked by a professional mechanic using a vehicle lift and special tools. Always refer to your owner's manual for specific instructions and recommendations for your make and model.

Power Steering Fluid

If the power steering fluid is low, it will need to be topped up. Checking the power steering fluid level is a straightforward process that should be done regularly to ensure your vehicle's power steering system is functioning properly. Here's how to do it:

• Park your car on a level surface and turn off the engine.

• Open the hood and locate the power steering fluid reservoir. It's usually located near the power steering pump on the engine, and it may have a label or a steering wheel symbol on the cap.

• Check the fluid level: If the reservoir is translucent, you can check the level visually. The fluid should be between the "MIN" and "MAX" lines on the reservoir. If the reservoir is opaque, remove the cap and check the level using the dipstick attached to the cap. The fluid should be between the "MIN" and "MAX" marks on the dipstick.

• If the fluid level is low, add the recommended power steering fluid for your vehicle (check your owner's manual). Use a funnel to avoid spills and be careful not to overfill.

• If the fluid appears dark, cloudy, or has a burnt smell, it may be contaminated and should be replaced. In this case, it's best to have the system inspected by a professional mechanic.

• After adding fluid or checking the level, replace the cap securely and close the hood.

• Start the engine and turn the steering wheel from lock to lock a few times to circulate the fluid. Check for any leaks or unusual noises.

If you notice that your power steering fluid level is consistently low or a leak is discovered, have your vehicle inspected by a professional mechanic. Always consult your vehicle's owner's manual for specific instructions and safety precautions related to your make and model.

Tire Inspection and Pressure

Your vehicle's tires will need to be checked for air pressure, tread depth, wear patterns, cuts, bulges, or other signs of damage. This includes the spare tire as well. If the air pressure is low, it must be adjusted to the recommended pressure levels for your vehicle and load conditions. Doing these checks regularly ensures safety, optimizes fuel efficiency, and extends the life of your tires. Here's how to check your car's tire air pressure:

- Obtain a tire pressure gauge. You can find one at most gas stations or auto parts stores.
- Check the recommended tire pressure for your vehicle. This information can be found in your owner's manual, on the driver's side door, or inside the fuel filler flap.
- Ensure your tires are cold, meaning the vehicle has been parked for at least three hours or hasn't been driven more than a mile.
- Remove the valve cap from the tire and place it somewhere safe, so you don't lose it.
- Press the tire pressure gauge firmly onto the valve stem. You may hear a brief hiss of air escaping while you do this.
- Read the pressure on the gauge. It will be measured in PSI (pounds per square inch) or BAR (barometric pressure).
- Compare the measured pressure to the recommended pressure. If the pressure is lower than recommended, add air to the tire using an air compressor. If the pressure is higher than recommended, press the center pin on the valve stem to release air until you reach the correct pressure.
- Replace the valve cap securely to prevent dirt and moisture from entering the valve.
- Repeat the process for all four tires, plus the spare tire if your vehicle has one.

It's important to check your tire pressure at least once a month and before long trips. Properly inflated tires provide better handling, improved fuel efficiency, and longer tire life. If you notice that one or more of your tires consistently loses pressure, have them inspected by a professional for potential leaks or damage.

Additionally, you should rotate your tires according to the manufacturer's recommendations, usually every 5,000-8,000 miles (8,000-12,800 km).

Brakes

Checking your car brakes regularly is crucial for ensuring your safety on the road. Check the thickness of the brake pads and replace them if they're worn down to the minimum recommended thickness. Inspect the brake rotors for excessive wear, grooves, or warping, and replace them if necessary. Keep track of the brake fluid level and condition. If necessary, replace the fluid if it appears contaminated or has absorbed moisture. Here are some additional steps to help you check your car brakes:

• Visually inspect brake pads: Look through the wheel spokes to check the brake pad thickness. If the pads appear to be less than 1/4 inch thick, they may need to be replaced. If you can't see the brake pads, consult a professional mechanic.
• Listen for unusual sounds: When applying the brakes, listen for squealing, grinding, or clicking noises, which may indicate worn brake pads or other issues.
• Feel for vibrations or pulsations: If you feel vibrations or pulsations in the brake pedal or steering wheel while braking, it could indicate warped rotors or other problems.
• Check the brake fluid level: Locate the brake fluid reservoir under the hood and ensure the fluid level is between the "MIN" and "MAX" marks. If the level is low, top it off with the recommended brake fluid and check for leaks.
• Test the parking brake: Engage the parking brake and ensure it holds the car securely on an incline.
• Notice changes in brake performance: If your brakes feel spongy, require more effort to press, or if the car pulls to one side while braking, it could indicate a problem.
• Schedule regular brake inspections: Have a professional mechanic inspect your brakes at least once a year or according to your vehicle's maintenance schedule.

If you notice any issues with your brakes or are unsure about their condition, have them checked by a qualified mechanic as soon as possible. Brake problems can compromise your safety and should be addressed promptly.

Lights

Check all exterior lights (headlights, taillights, turn signals, brake lights, and reverse lights) to ensure they are functioning correctly. Replace any burnt-out bulbs or faulty lamps. Clean the lenses and reflectors to ensure optimal visibility. If the light cover is cracked or broken, be sure to replace it as well. Here's how to check each light system for your car:

Headlights

• Turn on your headlights and walk around to the front of the car to ensure both low and high beams are working.
• Check for any dimming, flickering, or misaligned lights.

Taillights

• Turn on your headlights (which will also turn on your taillights) and walk to the back of the car.
• Check that both taillights are illuminated and not dimming or flickering.

Turn Signal Lights

• Turn on your hazard lights and walk around the car to check that all four turn signals (two in front, two in back) are blinking.
• Alternatively, have someone watch the lights as you activate the left and right turn signals from inside the car.

Brake Lights

• Ask a friend to stand behind the car as you press the brake pedal.
• Ensure all brake lights (usually three - two on the sides and one in the center) illuminate when the pedal is pressed.

Reverse Lights

• With your friend still standing behind the car, shift into reverse gear.
• The reverse lights (usually two, one on each side) should illuminate.
If you notice any lights not working, dimming, flickering, or appearing misaligned, replace the bulbs or have your car inspected by a mechanic. It's important to address these issues promptly, as non-functioning lights can compromise your safety and may result in a traffic violation.

Some newer cars have LED lights or more complex lighting systems. In these cases, consult your owner's manual for specific instructions on checking and replacing lights, or have them inspected by a professional.

Air Filter

Replace the engine air filter according to the manufacturer's recommendations or when it appears excessively dirty. This is a simple maintenance task that can improve your vehicle's performance and fuel efficiency. A clogged air filter can have the opposite effect. Here's a step-by-step guide on how to replace a car air filter:

• Locate the air filter housing: Open your car's hood and locate the air filter housing. It's usually a large, black plastic box near the engine, with a hose running from it to the engine intake. If you're unsure, consult your vehicle's owner's manual for the exact location.
• Remove the old air filter: Unclip or unscrew the fasteners holding the air filter housing cover in place. Remove the cover and take out the old air filter. Note the direction of the filter to ensure you install the new one correctly.
• Clean the housing: Use a vacuum or clean cloth to remove any dirt or debris from inside the air filter housing. Be careful not to let any debris fall into the engine intake.
• Insert the new air filter: Compare the new filter to the old one to ensure it's the correct size and shape. Place the new filter into the housing, making sure it

sits securely and is facing the correct direction (usually with the rubber seal facing towards the engine).

• Replace the cover: Put the air filter housing cover back in place and secure it with the fasteners. Make sure the cover is properly seated and all fasteners are tight.

• Close the hood: Double-check that the air filter housing cover is securely in place, then close the hood.

It's recommended to replace your car's air filter every 15,000 to 30,000 miles, depending on your driving conditions and vehicle manufacturer's recommendations. Check your owner's manual for the specific interval for your vehicle. If you frequently drive in dusty or polluted conditions, you may need to replace your air filter more often. A dirty or clogged air filter can reduce engine performance and fuel efficiency.

Battery

Check the battery terminals for corrosion and clean them if necessary. Next, ensure the battery is securely mounted and the connections are tight. And finally, test the battery with a voltmeter or load tester to check its condition and charge level. If your battery needs to be replaced, this can be done with minimal tools. Here's a step-by-step guide on how to replace a car battery:

• Safety first: Put on protective gloves and eye wear, turn off the engine, and remove the key from the ignition.

• Locate the battery: Open the hood and locate the battery. It's usually in a corner of the engine compartment.

• Disconnect the negative (-) cable: Use a wrench to loosen the nut on the negative (-) battery cable clamp, which is usually black. Carefully remove the cable from the negative battery terminal and set it aside, ensuring it doesn't touch any metal parts.

• Disconnect the positive (+) cable: Use a wrench to loosen the nut on the positive (+) battery cable clamp, which is usually red. Carefully remove the cable from the positive battery terminal.

• Remove the old battery: Unfasten the clamp or strap holding the battery in place. Carefully lift the old battery out of the tray.

• Clean the battery tray: Use a wire brush and a mixture of baking soda and water to clean any corrosion from the battery tray and cable clamps.

• Install the new battery: Place the new battery in the tray, ensuring it's facing the right direction (terminals should match cable positions). Secure the battery

with the clamp or strap.
• Reconnect the positive (+) cable: Connect the positive cable to the posi-tive battery terminal and tighten the nut securely.
• Reconnect the negative (-) cable: Connect the negative cable to the nega-tive battery terminal and tighten the nut securely.
• Test and clean up: Start the car to ensure the battery is correctly installed and working. Close the hood and dispose of the old battery properly (most auto parts stores will recycle it).

Always consult your vehicle's owner's manual for specific instructions, as some cars may have special steps or tools required. If you're unsure about the process, it's best to have the battery replaced by a professional mechan-ic.

Windshield Wipers and Washers

Replace the wiper blades when they start streaking or leaving gaps on the windshield. Check the windshield washer fluid level and top it up with the recommended solution. This can greatly improve visibility during rainy or snowy conditions. Here's a step-by-step guide on how to replace windshield wipers:

• Choose the correct wiper blades: Consult your vehicle's owner's manual or check the size of your current wiper blades to ensure you purchase the correct replacements. Wiper blades come in various lengths and attachment styles, so make sure you get the right ones for your car.
• Lift the wiper arms: Turn off the engine and lift the windshield wiper arms away from the windshield until they lock in the upright position.
• Remove the old wiper blades: Locate the small tab or button on the under-side of the wiper blade, where it meets the wiper arm. Press the tab and slide the blade down and out of the hook on the arm. Some blades may require you to press the tab and pull the blade in the opposite direction. Repeat this process for the other wiper blade.
• Attach the new wiper blades: Remove the new wiper blades from their packaging. Align the new blade with the hook on the wiper arm and slide it in the opposite direction of how you removed the old blade until it clicks into place. Repeat this process for the other wiper blade.
• Test and adjust: Gently lower the wiper arms back onto the windshield. Turn on the wipers to ensure they are securely attached and functioning properly. If necessary, adjust the angle of the wiper blades so they make full

contact with the windshield.

It's recommended to replace your windshield wipers every 6 to 12 months, or whenever you notice they are not effectively cleaning your windshield. Worn or damaged wiper blades can streak, smear, or miss areas of the windshield, compromising visibility in poor weather conditions. Some wiper blades may have slightly different attachment mechanisms, so always refer to the instructions provided with your new blades or consult your vehicle's owner's manual for specific guidance.

Additionally, it's essential to follow the manufacturer's recommended maintenance schedule for your specific vehicle model and driving conditions. Regular maintenance not only helps ensure your vehicle's reliability and safety but can also extend its lifespan and improve fuel efficiency.

Emergency Vehicle Repairs

There will be times where you will be in a situation with your vehicle where you must urgently tend to it. Otherwise, you will be stranded in the middle of nowhere if you're away from your home or unable to leave your home if you are at home. Here are some of the more common issues when dealing with inoperable vehicles:

Breakdowns

Dealing with breakdowns can be stressful, but having the knowledge and proper tools during these times can help you handle the situation more effectively. Here's some guidance on how to deal with flat tires, engine overheating, and battery issues:

Flat Tire

First, pull over to a safe location, away from traffic, and turn on your hazard lights. If you have a spare tire and the necessary tools (jack, lug wrench), follow these steps:

- Loosen the lug nuts of the flat tire before jacking up the vehicle.
- Position the jack properly according to the manufacturer's instructions.
- Fully remove the lug nuts and flat tire, then mount the spare tire.
- Lower the vehicle and tighten the lug nuts in a star or crisscross pattern.

If you don't have a spare tire or the necessary tools, call for roadside assistance

or a tow truck.

Engine Overheating

Pull over to a safe location and turn off the engine. Do not open the radiator cap while the engine is hot, as the hot coolant can cause severe burns. Once the engine has cooled down, check the coolant level in the radiator or overflow tank. If the coolant level is low, add more coolant or water (if coolant is unavailable) and check for any coolant leaks.

If the problem persists, it may indicate a more serious issue, such as a faulty water pump, thermostat, or radiator. In this case, call for roadside assistance or a tow truck.

Battery Issues

If your vehicle won't start due to a dead battery, you can try jump-starting it with a set of jumper cables and another vehicle with a charged battery.
• Park two vehicles close enough for the jumper cables to reach, but not touching.
• Connect the positive (red) cable to the positive (+) terminals of both batteries.
• Connect the negative (black) cable to the negative (-) terminal of the charged battery, then to an unpainted metal surface (e.g., engine block) on the vehicle with the dead battery.
• Start the vehicle with the charged battery and let it run for a few minutes, then try starting the second vehicle with the dead battery. If the dead battery vehicle starts, let it run for a while to recharge the battery before disconnecting the jumper cables in reverse order. If the battery is old or won't remain charged, it may need to be replaced.

It's always a good idea to carry a well-stocked emergency kit in your vehicle including a spare tire, jack, jumper cables, coolant, and other essential tools and supplies. Additionally, familiarize yourself with your vehicle's owner's manual for specific instructions and recommended procedures for dealing with breakdowns.

If you feel unsafe or unsure about attempting repairs, it's best to call for professional roadside assistance or a tow truck to avoid further damage or potential injuries.

Off-Road Driving Techniques and Safe Practices

When you are out in the mountains, woods, or desert, you will encounter driving conditions that might take a toll on your vehicle's exterior features and even interior parts. To ensure that your vehicle remains sturdy enough to withstand these conditions, keep in mind the following practices:

Certain road and weather conditions require extra caution when behind the wheel. Safety is critical for making it through rainstorms, ice, mud, snow, or wind. Here are some important tips for navigating such situations:

Vehicle Inspection

Before embarking on a journey through rough terrain, thoroughly inspect your vehicle to ensure it's in good working condition. Check the tires, brakes, suspension, and fluid levels. Be sure to carry essential supplies like a spare tire, jack, and recovery boards.

Tire Pressure

Proper tire pressure is crucial for maintaining traction on rough surfaces. In general, slightly deflating tires (within the recommended range) can improve grip on loose surfaces like sand, mud, or gravel. However, over-deflating can lead to tire damage or separation and must be avoided at all costs.

Speed Control

Maintain a slow and steady pace when driving on rough terrain or in adverse conditions. High speeds can cause you to lose control of your vehicle, potentially putting your life in harm's way. To remain in control, brake gently and avoid sudden acceleration or deceleration.

Terrain Analysis

Analysis of ground conditions involves looking for obstacles, steep inclines, or areas that may be too challenging for your vehicle's capabilities. If unsure, it's better to either find an alternate route or proceed on foot to assess the situation. Here are some other key factors to consider when analyzing terrain for driving:

- Type of surface: Identify the surface material, such as asphalt, concrete, gravel, sand, mud, or rocks. Different surfaces require different driving techniques and may affect traction, stability, and tire pressure.
- Incline and decline: Assess the steepness of hills or slopes in your path. Steep

inclines may require more power and momentum, while steep declines demand careful speed control and braking.

• Obstacles: Look for obstacles such as rocks, trees, logs, or deep ruts that could damage your vehicle or impede your progress. Plan your route to avoid or safely navigate around these obstacles.

• Water crossings: Note any water crossings, such as streams, rivers, or flooded areas. Consider the depth, current, and bottom surface of the water before attempting to cross.

• Traction: Evaluate the surface for potential traction issues, such as loose gravel, sand, or slippery mud. Adjust tire pressure, gear selection, and driving technique to maintain traction and control.

• Vehicle clearance: Be aware of your vehicle's ground clearance to avoid bottoming out on uneven terrain or high centering on obstacles. Choose a path that accommodates your vehicle's clearance capabilities.

• Weather conditions: Consider current and forecasted weather conditions that may affect the terrain, such as rain, snow, or extreme heat. Adjust your driving plan and techniques accordingly to maintain safety.

• Recovery points: Identify potential recovery points, such as level ground or sturdy trees, in case your vehicle becomes stuck or disabled. Carry appropriate recovery gear, such as tow straps, winches, or traction boards.

When analyzing terrain, it's essential to take a slow, methodical approach and make informed decisions based on your vehicle's capabilities and your own driving skills. If you're unsure about the safety of a particular route or obstacle, it's always best to err on the side of caution and find an alternative path.

Remember to comply with local laws and regulations, respect private property, and practice "Leave No Trace" principles to minimize environmental impact when driving off-road.

Traction Aids

Traction aids are devices or techniques used to improve a vehicle's grip on the road surface, especially in low-traction and slippery conditions such as snow, ice, and mud, or in high-traction conditions such as those involving loose gravel. Here are some common traction aids and how to use them:

Tire Chains

• Install tire chains on the drive wheels of your vehicle (front wheels for

front-wheel drive, rear wheels for rear-wheel drive, or all four wheels for all-wheel drive).

- Ensure the chains are properly sized and fitted for your tires.
- Drive slowly and avoid spinning the wheels, as this can damage the chains or your vehicle.

Snow Tires
- Replace your regular tires with snow tires during winter months or when driving in snowy conditions.
- Snow tires have special tread patterns and compounds that provide better traction on snow and ice.
- Ensure your snow tires are properly inflated and have sufficient tread depth.

Traction Control Systems
- Many modern vehicles are equipped with electronic traction control systems that automatically apply the brakes or reduce engine power to prevent wheel spin.
- Keep your traction control system turned on when driving in low-traction conditions.

All-wheel Drive (AWD) or Four-wheel Drive (4WD)
- If your vehicle has AWD or 4WD, engage the system when driving in low-traction conditions.
- These systems distribute power to all four wheels, providing better traction and stability.
- Remember that while AWD and 4WD improve traction, they do not improve braking or cornering abilities on slippery surfaces.

Sand/Traction Mats
- If your vehicle becomes stuck in snow, mud, or sand, place sand mats or traction mats in front of or behind the drive wheels.
- These mats provide a temporary surface for the tires to grip, allowing you to drive out of the stuck position.

Lower Tire Pressure
- In some off-road situations, such as driving on sand or deep snow, lowering your tire pressure can help improve traction by increasing the tire's contact

patch with the surface.
• Always reinflate your tires to the recommended pressure when returning to normal road conditions.

When using traction aids, always prioritize safety and follow the manufacturer's instructions. Adapt your driving style to the conditions, reducing speed and increasing distances as necessary. Remember that traction aids are not a substitute for safe, cautious driving and proper vehicle maintenance.

Hill Climbing and Descending

When navigating steep hills, it is important to use a low gear and maintain a steady speed. Always avoid stopping or changing gears on a hill, as this can result in a loss of momentum or traction. When descending, use engine braking and a low gear to control your speed. Remember, proper technique is essential for maintaining control and safety. Here's how to ascend and descend hills:

Ascending Hills

• Approach the hill at a steady speed, maintaining momentum without accelerating excessively.
• Select the appropriate gear before reaching the hill. For manual transmissions, use a lower gear to maintain power and control. For automatic transmissions, the vehicle should select the proper gear on its own.
• Maintain a constant speed as you climb, using the accelerator pedal to adjust speed as necessary.
• If the vehicle starts to lose power or speed, downshift to a lower gear to maintain momentum.
• Avoid stopping on a steep hill if possible. If you must stop, use the brake to hold the vehicle and then gently accelerate to start moving again.

Descending Hills

• As you approach the downhill slope, slow down and assess the steepness and length of the hill.
• Select a lower gear before descending. This helps control speed and reduces strain on the brakes.
• Use engine braking by gently releasing the accelerator and allowing the engine to slow you down.
• If needed, apply the brakes gently to maintain a safe speed. Avoid riding the brakes, as this can cause overheating and reduced effectiveness.

- Maintain a safe distance from vehicles ahead, as they may slow or stop unexpectedly.
- If your vehicle has a "hill descent control" feature, engage it as directed by the manual to automatically control speed on steep downhills.

Additional Tips
- Maintain a safe speed and avoid sudden acceleration or braking.
- Look ahead and anticipate changes in terrain.
- Be cautious and use lower gears if driving a heavily loaded vehicle.
- Reduce speed and increase following distance in slippery conditions like rain, snow or ice.
- If unsure about the terrain or your vehicle's capabilities, err on the side of caution and find an alternate route.

Safe hill driving requires a combination of proper technique, situational awareness, and good judgment. Always prioritize safety and adapt your driving to the conditions.

Water Crossings
Before attempting to cross a body of water, make sure to check the depth and the firmness of the seabed or floor. If possible, exit the vehicle and probe the area on foot. If the water is too deep or the current is too strong, it is advisable that you find an alternate route.

Crossing a body of water in a vehicle can be dangerous and should only be attempted with extreme caution and proper preparation. Here's how to safely cross a body of water in a vehicle:

Assess the Situation
- Determine the depth, width, and current of the water crossing.
- Check for submerged obstacles, such as rocks, logs, or holes.
- Ensure your vehicle has sufficient ground clearance and is equipped to handle the water crossing (e.g., a proper snorkel for the air intake, waterproofed electrical components).

Prepare your Vehicle
- Engage four-wheel drive (4WD) or all-wheel drive (AWD) if available.
- Lock the differential(s) if your vehicle is equipped with this feature.

- Close all windows, doors, and vents to prevent water from entering the vehicle.
- Disconnect or protect any electrical components that may be exposed to water.

Approach the Water Crossing

- Approach the water at a slow, steady speed to create a bow wave in front of the vehicle.
- Avoid creating a large splash or sudden changes in speed, as this can cause water to enter the engine compartment.

Maintain Momentum

- Once in the water, maintain a slow, steady speed to keep the bow wave in front of the vehicle.
- Avoid stopping or changing gears while in the water, as this can cause the vehicle to lose momentum and become stuck.

Monitor your Progress

- Keep an eye on your vehicle's temperature gauge to ensure the engine is not overheating.
- Watch for signs of water entering the vehicle or engine compartment.
- If the vehicle begins to drift or lose traction, gently steer in the direction of the current to maintain control.

Exit the Water Crossing

- Once you reach the other side, maintain momentum until you are fully out of the water.
- Check your brakes, as wet brakes may have reduced effectiveness. Gently apply the brakes a few times to dry them out.
- Inspect your vehicle for any signs of water damage or leaks.

Remember, if you are unsure about the safety of a water crossing, it is always best to find an alternative route. Water crossings can be unpredictable and can quickly lead to dangerous situations. Only attempt water crossings if you have the proper equipment, training, and experience.

Recovery Techniques

If the vehicle you are operating gets stuck, recovery boards and traction mats will help to dislodge your vehicle from the area in which it is stuck. You can also dig out the tires to regain traction. If necessary, use a winch or

seek assistance from another vehicle. Avoid spinning the wheels excessively, as this can deepen the hole even further.

Safety Equipment

Some essential safety items include a first-aid kit, fire extinguisher, emergency blankets, and communication devices like a satellite phone or radio.

Passenger Safety

Ensure that all passengers are buckled up with their seat belts properly secured. Avoid carrying more passengers than the vehicle can hold, as this can affect driving stability.

Remember, driving on rough terrain and in adverse conditions requires patience, skill, and a healthy respect for the environment. If a destination seems too risky or beyond your capabilities, it's always better to turn back or seek assistance rather than putting yourself or others in danger.

Conclusion

Whether you're preparing to bunker down inside your home or go out into the wilderness to live and thrive off of the land, all you need to be successful is the right preparation.

Preppers have always been ridiculed and joked about. They've been called doomsdayers and nutters, and plain crazy. However, if recent events have shown us anything they've shown us that there is nothing wrong with being prepared for the worst.

Go out there and stockpile to your heart's contents. Create a bug in plan, but always be ready to bug out when necessary. Train your body and your mind to survive the days where you don't have access to food or water or even electricity.

If an apocalypse does come, the ones that survive will be the ones that were prepared for it.

References

Arcuri, L. (2021, August 11). Sheep Are an Ideal Livestock Animal for a Small Farm. Treehugger. https://www.treehugger.com/how-to-raise-sheep-3016859

Baird, J. (2021, November 5). Three Proven Methods of Survival Fishing. Field & Stream. https://www.fieldandstream.com/survival/methods-of-fishing-for-survival

Centers, J. (2020, September 9). List of foods to buy from the supermarket for your prepper pantry. The Prepared. https://theprepared.com/homestead/guides/supermarket-food-list/

Channel, B. H. (2012). Greywater - recycling water at home. Vic.gov.au. https://www.betterhealth.vic.gov.au/health/HealthyLiving/greywater-recycling-water-at-home

College, S. (2021, February 11). From feed to fencing, here's what you need to know about raising goats. Treehugger. https://www.treehugger.com/how-to-raise-goats-3016858

Contributor, S. (2015, April 14). Homemade Booby Traps: Enter At Your Own Risk. Www.skilledsurvival.com. https://www.skilledsurvival.com/homemade-booby-traps-protect-home/

Dumbauld, B. (2019). Top 10 Outdoor Survival Tips. Nwtf.org. https://www.nwtf.org/hunt/article/ten-outdoor-survival-tips

Everet, W. (2021, December 27). 5 DIY Composting Toilet Ideas And Details To Consider • Insteading. Www.insteading.com. https://insteading.com/blog/diy-composting-toilet/

Garrett, B. (2020, May 3). We Should All Be Preppers. The Atlantic. https://www.theatlantic.com/ideas/archive/2020/05/we-should-all-be-preppers/611074/

Heritage, C. (2019, November 13). What Is A Septic Tank & How Does One Work? | D-tox. Www.dtox.org. https://www.dtox.org/blog/what-is-a-septic-tank-and-how-does-it-work

Idris. (2021, December 24). Open Air Composting: Step By Step Guide - Web-gardener - Gardening and Landscaping Made Simple. Www.webgardner.com. https://www.webgardner.com/composting/open-air-composting-step-by-step-guide/

Jane, O. (2020, March 10). 13 Tips for Window Security. WCMA - Window Covering Manufacturers. https://www.wcmanet.org/window-security/

Jessica. (2019, January 2). EASY HOMEMADE BREAD RECIPE. Butter with a Side of Bread. https://butterwithasideofbread.com/homemade-bread/

McEntire, K. (2021, November 16). How to Secure a Front Door. SafeWise. https://www.safewise.com/resources/how-to-guide-door-security/

McKenzie, C. C. (2021, June 23). How to Raise Happy Chickens. Country Living. https://www.countryliving.com/life/kids-pets/a32102474/raising-chickens/

News, M. E. (2021, December 30). The Guide to Raising and Breeding Rabbits for Meat – Mother Earth News. Www.motherearthnews.com. https://www.motherearthnews.com/homesteading-and-livestock/breeding-rabbits-zmaz70mazglo/

Preppers, F. (n.d.). Freedom Preppers | hunting for preppers for Preppers. Www.freedompreppers.com. Retrieved April 15, 2022, from http://www.freedompreppers.com/hunting-for-preppers.htm

Schipani, S. (2019, June 19). 12 things to know about raising cows. Hello Homestead. https://hellohomestead.com/12-things-to-know-about-raising-cows/

Solutions, D. C. (2018, May 29). 8 Methods of Composting. Direct Compost Solutions. https://directcompostsolutions.com.au/8-methods-composting/

Survival, D., Passion, B. P. S. N. O. B. a, of, it should be a lifestyle T. definition of a prepper is "An individual or group that prepares or makes preparations in advance, To, O. P., Circumstances, A. C. in N., Government, without substantial resources from outside sources" L. the, Plus, police etc I. don't believe that the end of the world will be the "end of the world" I. believe it will be the end of the world as we know it now Y. can also find me on G., & Twitter. (2019, April 11). Home Defense Tactics & Home Security. Survivalist Prepper. https://survivalistprepper.net/home-defense-tactics-home-security/

Vuković, D. (2019a, January 10). Best Prepper Foods You Can Find in the Supermarket. Primal Survivor. https://www.primalsurvivor.net/prepper-foods/

Vuković, D. (2019b, August 16). How To Build A Survival Shelter: 11 Simple Designs. Primal Survivor. https://www.primalsurvivor.net/wilderness-survival-shelter-no-supplies/

Zitzman, L. (2020, July 20). How to Build an Underground Bunker in 9 Steps | BigRentz. Https://Www.bigrentz.com. https://www.bigrentz.com/blog/how-to-buildHA-underground-bunker

Made in the USA
Las Vegas, NV
05 October 2024

96302713R10195